WE FELL ON STONY GROUND

WE FELL ON STONY GROUND

Edwin L Robinson

The Book Guild Ltd
Sussex, England

The Book Guild Ltd.
25 High Street,
Lewes, Sussex

First published 1998
© Edwin L. Robinson, 1998

Set in Times
Typesetting by Acorn Bookwork, Salisbury, Wiltshire

Printed in Great Britain by
Bookcraft (Bath) Ltd, Avon

A catalogue record for this book is
available from the British Library

ISBN 1 85776 239 8

*To Linda my wife, our three sons,
three daughters-in-law, seven grandchildren.
A window on my salad years.*

CONTENTS

CONTENTS

1

1942: A Voyage Round Africa

1942 dawned with the promise of travel, perhaps real action. The 11th Armoured Division, to which I had recently been posted, was being dismembered, its parts being attached to other more needy operational formations overseas, now that the intended invasion by Germany of the United Kingdom had failed.

Individuals too, like pieces in a game of chess, were moved to new positions. Myself, as one of the Superintendants at Northern Command Communication Centre (NORCO) during the Battle of Britain and the threat of invasion during 1941, landed a position as troop sergeant in a signals unit in limbo. The troop was billeted in a house called Sandylands near Egham in Surrey. The house was big enough to accommodate all 81 men of the troop, with room to spare.

The troop had been part of the 11th Armoured Division Head Quarter Signals and wore that formation's insignia: a black charging bull on a yellow background, whereas I wore the 'green apple' of NORCO. What else could be more appropriate in this 'ole boy's game? (The General's name was Adams.) Now stripped of our respective identities, we were earmarked to join another Armoured Division overseas, but they didn't say where.

As the only professional soldier in the troop of conscripted men between the ages of 20 and 23 (I was 25), with all the qualifications in radio, line and visual communications, and possibly the only one to have travelled and served overseas or even left home before 1939, it became my responsibility to keep the section fit, informed and above all, in touch with the realities of war; to stay alive and be aware of nature's gifts to

1

help them to stay that way. Apart from just taking cover from direct enemy action, there were the human pitfalls as well; most of the troop had lived cocooned by Victorian morals and were totally ignorant of the life they were soon to encounter beyond the shores of this class-divided country.

Subjects I felt compelled to discuss covered: venereal diseases such as gonorrhoea and syphilis, their recognition, prevention and early treatment; malaria, its cause, control and prevention; and typhus. These were the most prevalent diseases among soldiers serving in Britain's far flung Empire, and were discussed on a regular basis while I had been serving in India.

I also told them of the problems caused by dust on open wounds, on guns (large and small), and on electrical equipment, that could put the soldier, his weapon and means of communication out of action. I told them about the long distances that may have to be travelled without the convenience of petrol stations and corner shops. I hoped much of these talks and subsequent discussions, even though delivered by a humble sergeant, would be remembered. I think they were.

On Wednesday 11 February 1942 the whole signal unit (about 500 strong) received orders to be ready to move at 9.30 a.m. the following day. This called for a farewell party to which most of the troop attended at the 'Catherine Wheel' pub in Egham, complete with our two officers. The lads had brought along their newly acquired girlfriends. By closing time there were some misunderstandings as to who came with whom. Nothing serious though, nothing that by tomorrow would not be forgotten. By 1 a.m. and after three troop sergeants had carried out a bed check and reported all safely tucked in, I finally got my head down.

From 6 a.m. everyone seemed to understand the urgency to leave blankets, mattresses, furniture and rooms ready for the next occupants by 9.30. A lorry pulled in, all kitbags were loaded and the lorry left to collect from other billets, while we set off on a two-and-a-half mile march to Egham railway station. On arrival the station was packed with soldiers and civilians. It seemed as if half the town had turned out to see the lads off, although the move was supposed to be secret! All over the UK, in all public buildings, notices could be seen extolling the need for secrecy with the words 'Walls have Ears' hoping some might read them.

As the train pulled in a transport officer informed an inquiring officer: 'You will be on the train all night, arriving in Scotland in the early hours'. There was no general announcement to this effect – no walls – just a slip of the tongue.

Carriages had been allotted, and all that remained was to find the one assigned to my troop and pile in, informing them to settle down for the night. The train was named 'Remembrance'. First stop Leicester, then York where we were able to stretch our legs and where the Womens Voluntary Service (WVS) handed out sandwiches and tea. They seemed to be everywhere, God bless 'em.

The night passed without any hitch except that the water ran out and the smell of sweaty feet did nothing to improve the already stuffy atmosphere. Around 5 a.m. the train pulled into Edinburgh and without stopping moved on to Glasgow to be shunted to a siding alongside the King George 5th dock. Without ceremony each troop lined up to be counted, just in case someone decided to jump train. Each section or troop were served a good breakfast and issued with instructions stating which deck was to be their home and how to get there, even specifying which table on that mess deck.

It was good organization on the part of the embarkation authorities to place about 4,000 men in the grey tub tied up facing us, named *Nea Hellas*. The more knowledgeable among us knew its recent history. It had originally been called SS *Tuscania*, a cruise liner that had been sold to a Greek shipping company. But alas! Greece had fallen to the Axis forces. Its merchant ships if in Greek ports were the spoils of the conquering nation. Those still on the high seas were hijacked by others – this one, apparently, by the British Navy. It was a good story that came off someone's cuff.

The two gangways leading up to the ship were full with

3

heavily laden men in battle dress, a human trail that tailed back to the sidings and moved slowly into the ships bowels. Our troop, in four groups of 20, were guided down three decks to our allotted living space where the water lapped against the portholes. Each group commandeered a table, relieved themselves of their packs and looked around; 350 others were doing the same thing! Hooks attached to the beams six feet above the floor were for slinging hammocks and also to hang your equipment from. If you decided to wash your clothes, they too could hang on them. This was to be the lad's home for many weeks to come.

Grumbling started almost immediately. It was a difficult situation; troop ships were never built for comfort. I could only reiterate that everyone got very much the same first impression but as time went by, with full use of the upper decks, it would not be as bad as it seemed. With the help of other Non-Commissioned Officers (NCO's) of the troop the men were persuaded to store their backpacks and go on deck.

'Where are the Officers?' shouted a voice.

'Living it up in first class luxury' chorused a group. This of course was true, and in my opinion, though I did not express it, the extremes of privilege did irk relations between officer ranks and those of other ranks. Especially now, in an army comprised mainly of conscripted men herded together in conditions they had never envisaged. Tempers were bound to rise. It was not the first such situation I had experienced.

Even before the war the intelligence of enlisted men was continually rising in line with technical knowledge and the social gap narrowed as well. Now it was no longer the case that an order, right or wrong, *must* be obeyed. Skilled engineers, motor engineers and mechanics, radio operators and a host of other skilled men filled the ranks from private to general and orders likely to do more harm than good were disputed. The army, due to technical advances, required high standards to match that of the adversary. NORCO was manned by soldiers who had maintained the nation's public service industries prior to any declaration of war. This troop was of the same calibre.

4

As darkness fell on the evening of Friday, 13 February tempers had cooled as hammocks and sandwich packs were handed out and gangways sealed off. Those onboard found a place to sleep, either on deck or below. Those on shore found space in the sheds. What struck me as odd was that there was no public address system.

About 11 a.m. on 14 February the last of the draft had come aboard, filling every crevice of the ships innards. This crowding, for many reasons, must have scared the daylights out of some. Few, if any, realized the surge of anger, coupled with panic, that erupted in spontaneous action as preparations for cast-off were in progress. All that remained was the removal of the gangways. In fact, the forward gangway was already being lowered.

There remains impressed on my mind a memory of a scene I looked down on from the deck above the aft gangway. A small group rushed the Redcaps (military police), others pushed them back, seemingly out of harms way, to allow the stampede that followed.

A group of military police on shore saw what was happening and ran with their captain to the foot of the gangway. The Captain, a big fellow, continued up the gangway to stem the downward rush, meeting head-on with those going down; fists, boots and weight forced the Captain aside. He had lost his swagger stick, and at one point he was leaning backwards over the rail, and it looked as if he might follow it into the drink. In fact that is where the Captain would have ended up had it not been for the desperate efforts on the part of his own men to rescue him.

It was estimated 700 to 1000 soldiers had got ashore before the stampede was halted. No one on shore made a run for it. Someone from the ship called down and a Lance Corporal came to the front saying, 'We want better accommodation,' and then addressed those on the dockside. The authorities made no visual attempts to do anything.

The lull that followed left me uneasy as to what would happen next. A rumour circulated that machine-guns had been called for. If this were true, it would be the normal

5

reaction of the 'Captain Bloods' that might exist among the officer ranks to use them. Who ever was organizing this affair from the ship had calculated for this eventuality, for the word got around that the armoury was sealed off.

Suddenly, there, standing on a lifeboat high above the scene, stood a Corporal calling for order; what's more, he got it, from the ship and the shore. Then he pronounced, 'I have spoken to the officer in command of troops, to the embarkation officer, and the ship's medical officer, who are going to do everything that is possible for you. Meanwhile don't make any demonstrations but stay where you are until something is done'. Then he disappeared from my view.

I spotted my troop officer, a Captain, and together we searched the faces on the quay but could not recognize anyone from our unit. At the same time officers had been ordered to go ashore and mingle with the soldiers of their respective regiments. It was a good move as many were now engaged in earnest discussion. Eating humble pie by both sides resulted in a general return to the ship with the officers going below to see the conditions for themselves.

Our troop officer went off to collect the Second Lieutenant (second in command of the troop), and together we went below to have a chat with the lads assembled on the mess deck. The officers were rookies too, visibly embarrassed when they saw the difference: they in first class luxury while those they depended on to perform the duties assigned to the troop were crowded together on a deck below sea level. It was a situation about which they could do nothing; they had come face to face with an old British tradition, albeit outdated, that had existed from before the classic mutiny on HMS *Bounty* on 28 April 1789 provoked by the harsh treatment of the crew by its Captain. Today, the same thing was being played out on HMT *Nea Hellas*, provoked by harsh living conditions.

The only thing that could be said of this mutiny, if it could be described as such, was that it was treated by both sides with the utmost understanding. Times, in this respect, had changed dramatically since that mutiny 150 years ago. Every enlisted member of the armed forces in 1942 had a right to vote and be heard in parliament. A right granted as recently as 1938.

The officers did their best to explain but really they cut no ice. They were shaken by the events of the day and to save further embarrassment I pointed out that we would be able to meet each day on 'boat stations'. Before our discussion ended the vibrations that ran through the ship meant we were on our way.

What the media made of this affair or what happened to the three or so who refused to return to the ship I have no idea. No action, to my knowledge, was taken against any soldier who took part in the demonstration. We remained virtually incommunicado for the next eight weeks, and if any were like me, never saw an English paper for the next three years.

My advice to the lads was that the best place to be when sailing out of port is on deck taking in the last glimpses of the home scene. The River Clyde offered a wealth of interest; the number of ships being built and the panorama of this industrial river was all absorbing, as we listened to a vociferous proud Scotsman who had served his apprenticeship on the Clyde. He kept up a running commentary until the ship reached the open sea to take up its appointed station, and dropped anchor.

Looking around, in all directions, ships could be seen lying at anchor. One could only speculate that such a large convoy meant a whole army group were here, bobbing up and down at the whim of Atlantic rollers. The scene was really awesome, not least because the whole made an attractive target for the German U-boat packs known to be on the prowl. The destroyer that sculled around then disappeared into the blue again, reminiscent of the 'thin red line' syndrome that gave an illusion of protection but was in fact no more than a cosmetic dressing.

On Monday 16 February, real protection sailed in among the convoy: the battle cruiser *Malaya*, the aircraft carriers *Formidable* and *Eagle* and took up position in line at what I

7

took to be the centre of the convoy. A group standing by the rails began to count the destroyers, and between us we counted nine. Around 6 p.m. we commenced our journey south, feeling a bit more comfortable with all that armour standing guard over us. Almost immediately a rumour was taking its course; the German fleet that had been bottled up in Brest had escaped and were heading up the north sea hugging the European coastline. True or false, some got excited about it. 'Maybe, we will see some action?', said someone. 'Don't be daft. They're nowhere near us' came the reply out of the darkness, followed by loud laughter, while another gave a geographical lesson.

Like any group of people herded together, routine jobs were allocated on the several notice boards that had appeared during the day. To my surprise and on the first sailing day, I had been detailed for duty as ship's orderly sergeant. Part of this detail was to accompany the ship's orderly officer wherever our presence was required – one being a must; to tour the mess decks during the midday meal. We were to meet on the first class deck.

When I arrived he said, in that stupid acquired accent, officers tend to use, 'Sergeant, shall we start at the sharp end and work back?' 'Pompous twit,' I thought. 'Yes Sir,' I replied. He was no more than 20 and unlikely to create much impression on this bunch of disgruntled soldiers.

Complete with clipboard I guided him down to the forward mess decks. What a sight! The place appeared to be littered with seasick men, the atmosphere was stifling and the whole place stinking of a foul mixture of vomit and food. Every table we approached was the same, and those unaffected by motion sickness swore and shouted questions at us.

'The officer, when asked a question, started off with: 'The answer to that one is...' At one table, a brawny soul said: 'Never mind the answer, what are you going to do about this?' He pointed to his plate of pea soup with a host of flea-like creatures floating on the surface. Before the officer could speak I chipped in to say: 'All the food on board has come from warehouses, the whole dry pea consignment has been found to be affected by the pea weevil which is not visible in its dehydrated state. It is unfortunate they only appear when cooked; they really are harmless.'

'Who says?' replied the brawny soul.

'Do as I have done. Speak to those in the galley, say the orderly officer sent you to enquire.'

A group had gathered, and trouble was not far away when the brawny soul said, 'All right, I will.'

That was the tone on every mess deck. Boy! Was I glad to surface on the aft deck. We just stood for a moment filling our lungs with fresh air. On our way back to the upper deck the Second Lieutenant, in a more normal voice, said: 'Well, sergeant, thank God that's over, we won't be called on to go through that again.' There was a lot of relief in those words. This officer's training had led him to believe every non-commissioned soldier would stand to attention, salute, and regard him in awe. Today he had been sworn at, and at times expected to be doused with the slop the ship's cook had served up as food. Before parting, I handed him the clipboard with one word: 'Discontentment'. Very politely he said, 'Thank you, sergeant.'

He to his luxury and I to the sergeants' mess wondering how to get something going. Deck sports or any other entertainment, but something had to be done and quick. That was my report to the sergeants.

In the sergeants' mess we were served the same food as the rest, but we were able to discuss the problems of general welfare and discontent, were able to reach out to every living soul on the ship. Each morning at boat stations we had the opportunity to talk to those with special qualities in singing, musical instruments, or comedy to suit all tastes. It was a great success.

During the days that followed as the convoy sailed south, tempers cooled, and motion sickness died down. Each day at 10 a.m. boat stations were made use of to plan events: talks; cinema; shooting; games of all kinds. The convoy was still sailing in dangerous waters, so life jackets had to be carried at all times and most soldiers slept fully dressed. Feelings against authority had passed their high point, though subsiding, discipline remained an issue to be treated with understanding by NCOs rather than commissioned officers.

In the absence of enemy action I read books from the library. I ploughed through *Maria Monk* and passed it on. The spectacle of planes taking off and landing was good to watch. Some pilots had problems. Five planes were lost in the first two weeks; four undershot and hit the edge of the flight deck and fell into the sea. One landed alright, but was caught in a gust of wind and blown off the flight deck. On each occasion an escorting destroyer buzzed in to rescue the pilot.

In the evenings, with blackout regulations strictly enforced, life below decks continued as in pubs, without, of course, female company. There was a contingent of the Women's Royal Naval Service (WRNS) on board but hanky panky below decks was forbidden. They were to be found in areas where lighter social gatherings took place and where 'roughnecks' were discouraged. Walking round the darkened open decks it was not unusual to come across men in training. Skipping, boxing, weight lifting, anything that did not require space. The equipment was supplied from the ship's store. In a sheltered nook I glimpsed a dim light, surrounded by a group placing bets on a Crown and Anchor board. In a lighted corner on a mess deck table 'Pontoon' schools were the centre of attraction.

More up-beat forms of entertainment came from impromptu band concerts, by men brought together by the concerted efforts of officers and NCOs and enjoyed by both sexes. The warm balmy evenings fostered romance by the time our ship sailed into Freetown, the capital city of Sierra Leone. The name had been handed down from a fifteenth-century Portuguese Captain. While charting the west coast of Africa he had said he could hear the lions roar in the hills at night. I suppose the literal translation could be 'Lion Hills'. Sierra Leone sounds better though. Sierra Leone was colonized by the British with slaves repatriated from the UK and America from 1787 onwards. Most of the slaves were Christian and continued in that faith. In 1896 it became a British

10

protectorate, and now boasted of a deep-water harbour, a civil and military airport and a small garrison, and was a port of call for British ships sailing round the Cape.

The *Nea Hellas* and one other ship remained anchored in the harbour for six days. Each day groups of WRENS went ashore to join in the entertainment laid on there. There was no shore leave for the troops. The reason given: yellow fever. The ship was visited by the air officer commanding military personnel in west Africa. We were kept hanging around on boat stations for more than two hours. When he did arrive, he never said a word but seemed in a hurry and keen to get off this ship.

Bum boats (home made floating vessels) laden with fruit or trinkets surrounded the ship each day and did a good trade by means of rope and basket. Some were distinctly unseaworthy as they plied their trade. On one choppy-sea day, water slopped over the gunnels of one such a craft. The crew of two frantically tried to keep afloat by baling out with little tin pots. A naval launch went by, and its wash filled a boat that sank immediately. The crew made a dive for the nearest bum boat and tried to scramble on. A free fight took place in a desperate effort to prevent them boarding. Alas the crew could not bale out and fight as well, and so gave way to allow the invaders to help bale out, as they were now in peril themselves. The naval launch came by once more. The sailors were oblivious to the havoc they had caused to the first boat couldn't care less about what was happening on the second boat. With four adults on board, the wash from the launch was too much. The boat began to sink. The crews of two other bum boats saw what was happening and decided to head for the shore.

All eyes were focused on the sinking boat. Not only were there four adults aboard, but two small children appeared from a pile of sacking and began to cry while the crew baled to no avail. The naval launch, on its way to the shore, would have continued had not the troops shouted for them to return. After what seemed to be a dispute on the launch, it turned and drew alongside. The crew on the sinking bum boat

11

jumped for the launch, leaving the children behind. Without the adults, the bum boat righted itself and two little faces looked up at us. Someone threw a rope down which they clung to and were pulled in to the launch's side. A loud cheer went up – the children must have guessed it was for them. Their little hands reached out for the safety rope fixed to the ship, just above the water line. As if in acknowledgement to the cheering they looked up and smiled. A sailor lifted them to the safety of the launch and set off for the shore. I was not alone in wondering if they (the children) would survive to follow in their parents footsteps.

Freetown is about eight degrees north of the equator, with temperatures around 30°C, but the evenings were cool and orders to don our tropical uniform were welcomed. The shorts and topees looked shabby, and most decided to wear blue gym shorts and many topees were thrown over the side.

On the morning of 6 March we set sail from Sierra Leone. It was rumoured (we *lived* on rumour) that a pack of enemy U-boats were lying in wait. The only thing that hit us was a dose of diarrhoea that affected half the ship's human cargo. The torment lasted for at least a week, to some extent spoiling the 'mumbo jumbo' ceremony of crossing the equator. Spells of torrential rain were welcome gifts from the skies, to bathe, frolic and wash away the evil bug that made life a misery.

As the days passed, small groups were introduced to automatic weapons by the ships armourer. The blackout regulations had been lifted, and many attended to their uniforms as shore leave had been promised on arrival in South Africa. Good food was looked forward to, also a chance to get away from this ship we had come to detest.

At dawn on 18 March land was sighted. After breakfast we remained on deck as the ship sailed slowly past those peaks called the Twelve Apostles, Table Mountain, the Lions Head, and then we were in sight of Cape Town itself nestling at the base of a breathtaking backdrop. The people flashed out their greetings with mirrors that sparkled like diamonds in the morning sun. That morning we received our pay, and few

12

went down for the midday meal, savouring the prospect of a meal on shore.

The ship tied up. Along the quay came two South African soldiers toward the gangway, scrutinized by us, wondering what rank they held as they looked so smart. They turned out to be privates. This made us feel self-conscious, with our shabby ill-fitting clothes made of the cheapest material. We could do nothing but grin and bear just another insult, until 5 p.m. The great moment had arrived as we stepped ashore. Our clothes no longer mattered for at the dock gates what a wonderful greeting awaited us; hundreds were there with cars, people willing to be guides.

In retrospect it would only be right to apologize to those citizens whose offer of goodwill was turned down. We were young, healthy and hungry for food, sex and fun. It was wonderful to walk down brightly-lit streets after two-and-a-half years of blacked out streets. To see shops full of goodies that were not available in the UK, to sing the latest songs while following the girls that led us to dance halls. Everything was free. To fall in love was no sin. I got feeling it was all stage-managed, because all the fun and games stopped dead on 11 p.m. and we were cleverly guided back to the ship by midnight, with many promising to meet the next day.

This went on for three days – leaving the ship at 10 a.m., returning at midnight. Not a word was mentioned about sailing. Few enquired; we were in dreamland, the war out of sight. Had we known that tomorrow the ship was due to sail and I would never see the girl again, I, and perhaps many more, would not have passed through those dock gates so willingly. Instead we clung to each other, whispering sweet nothings. Now it was time for the last kisses before parting she to her home and I, to check-in on board the *Nea Hellas*.

Next morning I felt cheated. The gangways were up and the ship ready for sailing but the girl's perfume lingered. My heart was heavy, my head full of thoughts of a life that might have been as the ship sailed out of harbour at midday.

Many now leaning against the rails, watching the flashing mirrors must have realised their true meaning. Hello!

13

Goodbye! Good Luck! The town's final flashes of farewell faded, and the mirrors seemed to whisper God Bless you.

With a lump in my throat I turned inward to stark reality. We resigned ourselves to the indignities of another world called *Nea Hellas*, and were awakened by the call to boat stations. The roll call revealed one Corporal from our troop was missing – one of three from the ship. Not bad, when you take into account all that temptation.

Discussion groups were set up to talk about South Africa. The question of 'segregation', which was all too obvious, when put to men who had never travelled far from home, received an overwhelming response. They did not like what they saw in bars, cafés and buses. Even the seats in the shaded parks were labelled 'whites only' or 'blacks only'. They also heard that South Africa was not alone among nations practising segregation: perhaps not so blatant as in South Africa and the United States of America, but there were parallels, just the same. Britain did not escape; life on this ship was exposed as an example, but not one to dwell on and soon moved to the wider social divisions in our society. Germany, currently, persecuting the Jewish race was something far worse than they had encountered in South Africa. The series was brought to a close on India's religious and social class distinctions. A consensus of opinion revealed that: 'segregation was worldwide, existing in many forms in the shadow of this global war.' We novices in worldly ways, gaining first-hand knowledge, were tomorrow's ambassadors.

On the horizon a hazy blue outline was the last sighting of South Africa as the convoy sailed east into the Indian Ocean, still unaware of our final destination. At this point it could have been Australia, India, the 14th Army in Burma, facing east, or the 8th Army in Egypt facing west. It might have been 10th Army on the Syrian Iraq–Iran borders facing north. God, this country of ours' had a lot on its plate. The future was certainly not ours to see.

The following day we joined other ships that had called in at Durban. Our escort had diminished to the cruiser *Newcastle* and two destroyers. The *Newcastle* cruised among

14

the convoy with its marine band playing a selection of popular tunes. It was a fine gesture that turned out to be a form of farewell, for that evening, pinned on the notice boards, was a message from its commander bidding all officers and men a safe passage to their destination.

Before departing the next morning, the *Newcastle* suddenly began firing. On the eastern horizon appeared a ship and all the cruisers' forward guns were letting fly. We had expected a few shots in return, but none came. The word was circulated that the stranger was an armed merchantman coming to join the convoy as far as Aden.

The food since Cape Town had improved, the canteens were replenished, looked cleaner and their stock in trade was more in keeping with popular choice. Those earlier days had not been forgotten; our world was settling down under its own volition, developing a social lifestyle of its own. Training for the ship's sports were now being taken seriously. On Sundays 2,000 voices joined in hymn singing. The padre, a singularly enterprising individual, had overcome those who had persistently interrupted his services by renderings of ribald ballads during his sermon or the reading of the lesson. He never lost his cool. By ignoring all interruptions and bad behaviour he had inspired his following to do the same. From boat stations to lunchtime, sailors, soldiers, airmen and womens' services of all ranks called for their favourite hymns. This man had won over their hearts and voices in a simple, unhurried way. A true chaplain; an asset to any god.

Life on board had changed dramatically on this leg of the journey. Officers, sergeants, Corporals and privates got together more often. Groups of minstrels, poets, and comedians travelled the ship to entertain.

There was an Australian on board, handed over by the South African authorities as a leftover from the last Australian draft to pass by. As a deserter he was held in the brig (prison). He established himself as ship's dhobi wallah (laundry man), employing some ten others. He also ran a type of casino deep in the ships bowels.

There existed phantom caterers that served the finest

15

sandwiches money could buy, at no fixed place or time. The whole of the lower decks provided them with all the lucrative business they needed. Wherever they went the Red Caps were sure to follow, for their source of supply was the first class kitchen, where the finest food was stored and cooked. A sample of the goodies available were on the previous day's menu. Here's a sample from an earlier day:

TUESDAY, 24TH FEBRUARY, 1942

BREAKFAST

Grapefruit
Oatmeal Porridge
Shredded Wheat – Rice Crispies
Grilled Maux Kippers
Boiled, Fried or Turned Egg
Corn Beef, Dry Hash
Grilled Empire Bacon and Ham
Salisbury Steak, Onion Gravy

COLD BUFFET

Dill Pickles and Relishes
Rolls – Bread
Marmalade Preserves
Tea – Coffee – Cocoa

LUNCH

Potage St. Germain
Spaghetti, Tomato Sauce
Beefsteak Saute, Bourgeoise
Boiled Haunch of Mutton, Onion sauce
Spring carrots in Cream
Boiled and Mashed Potatoes

COLD BUFFET

Roast Beef – London Brawn
Roast Lamb
Salads, Beetroot and Onion, Vegetables

16

Apple Sponge Pudding
Biscuits – Cheese – Coffee

DINNER

Consommé Fermiere, Fresh Haddock, Meuniere
Lamb Chops, Saratoga Chips
Roast Sirloin of Beef au Jus
Brussels Sprouts, Boiled and Roast Potatoes

COLD BUFFET

Roast Beef – York Ham – Oxford Prawn
Lettuce and Mixed Vegetables – Salad
Fruit Trifle – Oranges
Biscuits – Cheese – Coffee

One evening with a group of sergeants chatting on our mess deck, a commotion on the gangway attracted attention. Men were running, others were shouting. The first man came up, and in a good rugby fashion sent a haversack toward me. In a similar fashion I took it and passed it back out of sight. The second and third men did the same thing and were gone. Close behind were two Red Caps. 'Which way did they go?', panted the leader.

'That way,' said one, pointing to the doors that led out onto the dock. Not anxious to be caught with the loot whatever it may be, we waited. The Red Caps returned. 'The bastards got away,' said one as he descended the gangway stairs. 'We'll get those buggers yet,' said the younger of the two between his teeth and followed his senior.

Satisfied the coast was clear, the haversacks were opened. '*Voilà*,' was the surprised call of the one learning French. In his haversack was a joint of sizzling beef about eight pounds in weight. In the other two were freshly made loaves of bread complete with a bread knife. We returned to a quiet corner (there were six of us) to enjoy the windfall. Out of gratitude, we later placed the three empty haversacks at the head of the

17

gangway, one deck down.

Another popular attraction which drew a sizable crowd was the impromptu get togethers in the canteen after the bar had closed. These were usually presented by a bearded sailor who worked in the galley and didn't bother to change. He always appeared in the same torn, greasy, once white vest, with a pair of trousers to match. His arms bore the tattoos of a well-travelled son of the seven seas, but streaks of soot mixed with a variety of other kitchen ingredients tended to obscure these works of art. If these were his failings, his talent and personality shone like a star to those who made up his fan club. His stage was a table, from where he would announce the words of a song or ballad and school his audience in the unprintable chorus. His songs depicted the low life of the flesh pots of Panama, Shanghai, Singapore, Calcutta, Bombay and many other ports of call where vice rides high.

The ship's sports lasted three days, ending in the finals of tug of war on the day the ship crossed the equator on its northerly course. On 6 April we sailed into the gulf of Aden, the south-eastern entrance to the Red Sea.

The port of Aden became a freeport in 1850 after the British settled there by force of arms in 1839. It is situated in and is the capital town of South Yemen. With the passage of time and local squabbling became a British crown colony, remaining a refuelling and staging port on the Empire route via the Suez Canal.

Refuelling took 24 hours. During that time a contingent of RAF personnel disembarked to serve in this hot, dry and barren land. At anchor nearby lay an Australian ship taking their lads back home from Egypt. A small dinghy-type boat came alongside; at times like this anything that moves becomes a focus of interest to some. A gangplank was pushed out just above water level and down the plank walked our only 'jailbird'. Settling himself down in the dinghy with his baggage, the oarsman pulled out. A voice of recognition shouted, 'There goes Aussie'. It seemed the whole ship erupted with a loud cheers. I could see the look of surprise on the face of the oarsman, wondering who his passenger was, for he was cheered all the way, loaded with Pommie cash. Australia had got its wayward, enterprising son back.

Slowly the ship sailed out through the straights into the Red Sea. There was no mistaking where we were going; Egypt's western desert. We were due to arrive at Suez on 10 April. Preparations for disembarking got underway and the holds were opened for each unit to check their gear. This chore out of the way, we could relax. About 11.30 p.m. on the second day out of Aden, I lay flat out on my bunk reading, hoping the phantom would come our way. There was a loud bang and the ship appeared to stop still. I slid out of the end of my bunk, while others, just landed on the deck between the bunks. The alarm sounded and confusion reigned as close on 4,000 souls went for their life jackets and make for the gangways leading to their boat stations. Everyone knew the route by heart – it had been practised every day for eight weeks. NCOs manned the gangways to keep the flow moving, but it still took the best part of 30 minutes to clear the lower decks. Whatever happened did not matter, we had eight rafts, and allotted ten men to each and waited.

No order to abandon ship was given, but through the grapevine filtered the cause of the bang; the *Nea Hellas* had rammed another ship. The evidence came into view. The rammed ship, a quarter the size of ours, with its stern almost awash, seemed to be sinking. A signal lamp flashed in morse code, which most of the troop were able to read. 'Stand by can float will keep you informed'. There appeared to be no immediate danger to our ship, and the all clear was given around 2 a.m.

By daybreak the cargo ship had run aground. Its American crew on our ship informed us that they had recently unloaded a cargo of explosives. The *Nea Hellas* was shaken up as it slowly moved towards its destination, and the rumpus had put routine out. After breakfast I lay down in my bunk and dozed off. It must have been the smell of smoke that made me jump out and dash on deck. Smoke was belching out from the forward deck. A soldier with a guitar was leaning against the rails and strumming. 'I don't want to set the world on fire, I just want to start a flame in your heart' he sang. Further on there were soldiers laughing and joking as kitbags floated by. Reaching the forward deck a mixture of crew and soldiers had formed a chain and were passing kitbags from a hold to be thrown overboard. Some 1,000 bags ended up in the sea. The source of the fire located, a soggy pile of kitbags remained to receive further drenching as the deck timbers with lingering embers were quenched.

The ship anchored off port Tewfiq in the gulf of Suez about four in the afternoon. All ranks were ordered to boat stations as lighters (floating platforms) were to be used to disembark. The first to be filled did not suit the transport officer. He shouted, 'Come on you lot, there is room for another hundred'. Then he continued, 'What do you think this is, a picnic?' No one moved. Someone let off a resounding raspberry. There was loud laughter. The officer said no more. The lighter headed for the landing stage. When our turn came and before reaching the landing stage I looked back at the ship I would never forget; its flat nose told its own story.

Royal Army Service Corps lorries stood by, a sergeant calling for all kitbags to be put on. Those without replied, 'They are in the Red Sea,' more laughter. But were promised that those on the lorries would be delivered within 14 days.

The last of our unit came ashore as the sun went down. There was no twilight hour, only minutes before total darkness. We were a rag-tag lot as we entered the transit camp to be fed and bedded down in the sand. We had arrived in the Kingdom of Egypt wondering what this country had in store for us.

2

1942: Egypt – In Defence of the Suez Canal

April 12 1942 – our first dawn under Egyptian skies, surrounded by mile upon mile of sand. We breakfasted on porridge, two boiled eggs, bread and butter with jam or marmalade gritty with sand, washed down with pints of tea. With no time to waste, we marched the short distance to a railway station to board the third class carriages of the Egyptian State Railways. I did not see any of our officers. Waiting for us at the station were hawkers who boarded the train while it was moving, jumping on and off to allow others to take their place. The free riders went from carriage to carriage, ready to buy or sell anything from a toothbrush to a gold watch, and they gave the lads a sample of eastern enterprise.

On the way we met British lines men maintaining the telephone system. They seemed miles from anywhere. The train was going slow enough for hurried questions and answers. The usual 'What's it like out here?' 'Anyone from this or that town?' and so on; pleasant banter. The inevitable 'Where's this chap called Rommel?' (commander of Axis Forces in North Africa). 'Don't worry, you'll soon bump into him...' Laughter.

In 1914 Egypt became a British protectorate until 1936. With the crowning of King Farouk, Egypt became an independent country. Britain, with its Empire commitments, came to an agreement with the Egyptian government to retain the right to maintain and defend the Suez Canal.

Cairo, signposted *Le Caire*, came in sight. Without entering the city the train stopped near a fleet of lorries. Without any formality it was just climb aboard, but I managed to get my troop in consecutive lorries. Our next stop was the open desert and there were a few tents around for our immediate use. The area was without a tree, building of any kind or sign post – just sand. It was known as El Katatbar. I believed it to be the temporary home of the embryonic 10th Armoured Division. Surprisingly, water was laid on to a washstand. There were two kinds of toilet: the Desert Rose (a large funnel shaped object sticking out of the sand visible to all including passing local inhabitants on camels) and deep rectangular pits with a superstructure supporting poles on which to sit while performing the necessary regular body functions. Both were regarded by the local Bedouins as strange contraptions. From their chatter and laughter while riding by, they must have found a lot to talk about while squatting by their evening fires, passing the hooker round, puffing hash and telling tales of the pink-skinned crusaders who now occupied their land.

A lorry turned up. Tents were unloaded and distributed. A neighbouring armoured car regiment sent a team over with kitchen equipment and an assortment of rations. Our cooks got to work to rustle up a meal while the rest, with officers and sergeants, planned the layout of the camp. Office furniture, training-tent tables and chairs, dining tent, and so on. By nightfall everything appeared to be in position.

As we had no vehicles, radio sets or any temporary means of honing our technical standards by practice, duties were minimal. Just getting used to living in the desert and maintaining general hygiene was taken seriously. The Second Lieutenant and I attended a two-hour desert navigation course with a Corporal instructor from an armoured car regiment. That was the extent of our initial desert training.

The unit was now on its own. The journey from Egham, England, to Cairo, Egypt and that bloody ship became a memory. We were now masters of our own destiny as vehicles and equipment began to arrive including our kitbags. Requisitions were made of missing articles of clothing under the guidance of the Second Lieutenant who had lost everything except what he stood up in. To ease the situation, three-ton lorries were laid on each evening for a trip into Cairo, less than an hour's journey away.

Within a month of arriving in El Katatbar, our adjutant (a Captain) and myself were detailed to attend a court-martial. The Corporal who had jumped ship at Cape Town had arrived under guard. I asked to see him, but it was not allowed. In the court-martial tent I tried to explain the circumstances and his character. When I started, a voice from one of the many officers present said: 'Thank you sergeant, that will be all'. My presence was merely to identify him. I felt court-martials were usually stacked against the soldier. Whenever the subject of court-martials was brought up for discussion, the verdict was unanimous; it was well known that examples had to be set. You never stood a chance.

The desert was a harsh school where fundamentals had to be grasped quickly. With the arrival of our own vehicles, motorbikes and radio equipment the troop settled down to some real training. The despatch rider section soon became a non-starter. The desert was no place for lone riders, though I retained the motorbike allotted to me.

My job was to see that every man should have the opportunity to drive out into the desert and fire his rifle, something that many had never done. They also had to be able to cook and fend for themselves using the established sand and petrol fires with the minimum use of water. It was surprising how quickly the lads caught on and became self-reliant.

Although small prismatic compasses were issued, they could be easily lost, and they were not a general issue. This was my real contribution to the men's knowledge: the stars had served me as a natural navigation tool from my school days in the Himalaya Mountains to my time as a serving soldier in India.

At this latitude, roughly 30° north, the Pole Star (Polaris) was also approximately 30° above the horizon. The pointers, in the constellation Ursa Major, were not always visible. The constellation Cassiopeia, situated opposite Ursa Major also had the means of offering an alternative line should one or the other be out of sight. These were the main signposts during the hours of darkness to get one's bearings.

The desert was a wonderful classroom, the sand serving as a blackboard with a stick or bayonet serving as chalk, and the stars shining out from a black velvet sky. The sun rose almost dead on 6 a.m. in the east and set at 6 p.m. in the west. A stick stuck upright in the sand also served as a direction-finder and timekeeper during daylight. A compass may get you to a pin-point position, but reading nature's gifts would get you to safety.

All the men in my troop were 'militiamen': the 20–21-year-olds conscripted in 1939 to defend the realm and its territorial possessions. I 'one of the 22–24-year-olds selected in 1939' had been sent from India to 'instruct, coach and impart whatever we had learned in work and play' to the younger men. Those were the words used before sending us to England in June 1939 as Class 1 signalmen (i.e. technical private soldiers), to become sergeants within six months.

On 15 July 1939, 360,000 conscripted men congregated on various sites in the country to start training for war. My first assignment was to make sure 60 men, from many different backgrounds, learned to touch-type. Like it or nor, they had been 'earmarked' as future teleprinter operators in the Royal Corps of Signals. The fact that I had never, like them, had cause to use a typewriter, was of little concern. 'You have eight weeks in which each man should reach a standard speed of 30 words per minute. You will find everything you require in the typing tent.' So said our camp commandant (affectionately known as Daddy). 24 weeks later 180 men had been dispersed to signal units across the country. I had earned my stripes then, and went on as a sergeant to instruct young soldiers in the use of weapons and drill, and supervise them on general duties. Here in this barren land, training groups in everyday desert living, desert navigation, and the pitfalls of driving. It was so easy to find your vehicle axle-deep in the sand, needing to be dug out. All of this I hoped would help them come out of this conflict alive.

The desert had its wildlife, albeit suffering the rampaging of an alien army careering over its homeland. One creature, the jeboa (desert rat) lived underground, surfacing frequently to forage for beetles and, perhaps, scorpions that scurried about on the surface. The jeboa appeared to be a territorial animal that voiced its anger when its front door (a small hole in the ground) was covered. It would then hop round and round squeaking at every hop. Often a soldier would cover the hole with his boot for a bit of fun to watch its antics. Never afraid, the jeboa would dance around the person squeaking as if to tell the twit to shove off. This small creature was befriended by the soldiers, and caught the imagination of a commanding officer of one of the early armoured units serving in Egypt, and became the emblem of the 7th Armoured Division. Whereas the 10th Armoured Division's emblem was a red fox's head on a black background, and I cannot recall seeing it worn by anyone.

Then there were the flies, which was not surprising considering the western desert had become one big open toilet. Away from base camps, such as El Katatbar, there were no latrines. When in the desert, do as the Arabs do. Pick your spot, select suitably-sized stones, and settle down. There was no such thing as toilet paper. The sun and the diurnal change of the wind baked, swept or covered all forms of waste, lessening the chance of diseases. Despite natures efforts, flies congregated by the billion.

The desert was far from infertile. I had an opportunity to stop by a water tower to fill my water bottle, and saw that where water trickled out from its overflow pipe the sand was soaked, lush green grass grew. It struck me that in this barren land seeds lay dormant, and must have done so for thousands of years. Given the right conditions, this desert could yet bloom again.

A weekly paper called *The Crusader* was of general interest but I was yet to know the name of our divisional commander, let alone the army commander, until the 8th Army had reached a crisis situation. No one turned up to say 'hello' or welcome, to the land of the Egyptians. In early May we were paraded. The Duke of Gloucester, we were told, was coming to visit the troops. Why us? Forming a hollow square we

25

waited and waited for over an hour. Then we were invited to sit down, and waited another hour in the burning sun. The big moment arrived. Out of the blue came a car across the open sands, followed by a cloud of dust. It pulled up some distance from where we waited. The Duke stepped out, and walked a few paces toward the troops. A cameraman was there, and a few officers were buzzing around. When the cameraman was satisfied he had got the subject (the Duke) in focus with the troops in the background, he returned to the car, taking with him a comforting picture for the folks back home. I cannot recall the Duke saying anything, and from where I stood he was unrecognizable. We just happened to be the nearest troops to Cairo. This visit did not go down well and the soldiers complained bitterly. The lads in my troop were really annoyed, and it was only right the troop officer was made aware of their grievance at being used in this way. He was not pleased, but that was all the better, for he would have to report his troops' feelings to the Colonel.

After the Duke had gone, a medical team turned up looking for blood donors, offering a pint of stout for a pint of blood. Some thought it a fair exchange, while others preferred to keep what they had. Whether blood was given or not a sample was taken from each person and categorized on the spot. At another table we received a fibre disc complete with number, name and blood group (known as the dog tag). This tag, it was emphasized, must be worn at *all* times for your own good, in case you fall into enemy hands. No one mentioned its other purpose.

As we were never kept informed it was always a matter of follow the leader, always hoping at some point our purpose would become apparent. By late June every man had been given 10 days holiday in Cairo or Alexandria, where contact with other troops began to make us wonder what exactly was happening. Battle-hardened soldiers were easy to distinguish from new arrivals. Any effort at conversation usually started with: 'What circus are you with?'

By this time we had moved further into the desert. My motorbike had been discarded for a Bedford pickup in which

26

I had installed a commercial radio. It was from the BBC I learnt that a thousand miles away in Libya, Rommel was on the attack. Unprepared and ill equipped, our unit began moving west, parallel to the coast road. No one could mistake what was happening. What started as a trickle grew into a mile upon mile of vehicles, including tanks on transporters and lorries loaded with furniture, nose to tail heading for the Nile delta, in the opposite direction us.

My guess (guessing had become an art and the nearest thing to information) was that we were heading for Mersa Matruh, a coastal resort and supply base. We never got there; the order came to turn and head in the same direction as those on the coast road. We were now in full retreat.

Although our retreat was unhurried and some distance off the coast road, what armour we did have was attempting a rearguard action. We had actually reached the outskirts of Alexandria where shopkeepers were already flying the Swastika and the Italian flag. Who could blame them? They lived here.

The next day my troop were ordered into the desert to form part of a defence line. This could only mean we were to be used as infantry. It was nothing new for signal corps personnel to be used in a last-stand situation; we were trained like any other combat soldier, carried a rifle and knew how to use it. By the time we turned off the tarmac road it was dark. We kept in sight of each other's vehicle, and the rattle of machine gun fire could be heard. Suddenly the advance stopped. All hell broke out as the big guns around us opened up, and the barrage continued through the night. The dawn seemed too quiet. The lull as the early morning sun warmed the air gave us time in which to contemplate: had the Axis forces run out of petrol or ammo? Or could they take no more of the continuous bombing and shelling? The flags went up and it was time to brew up.

That last-stand to hold the line had been successful, and allowed the army time to muster more men to make it hold. Once again we were heading for the delta, and on the way I hitched up to an abandoned three-ton lorry and took it to a town called Damanhur where the vehicle was reclaimed by its owners. The news was not good, our General had been relieved by the Commander in Chief of the Middle East, who was now standing in as 8th Army commander; a shakeup of top brass was taking place, but somehow the rank and file remained remarkably calm. At times like this I wondered if they (the lesser ranks) even cared about what happened to the army or its Generals. We had not been taken into their confidence, so why should they care? One thing was certain, the average Egyptian didn't care either – they would be prepared to do business with any occupier.

Anyone who cared to take a serious look at the map of the Middle East would have understood why Mr Churchill, our Prime Minister at the time, felt so concerned over the state of the 8th Army in July 1942. Around 80,000 were killed, wounded, or taken prisoner during the retreat from Libya and now those in authority were talking about retreating into Palestine.

The BBC news broadcasts told us that Mussolini, the Italian Supremo, had arrived in North Africa in preparation for a triumphal entry into Cairo to add Egypt to his North African empire. This was disconcerting enough, but looking north to Syria, Iraq and Persia (the northern front line), we realized our 10th Army would be no match against the 1st and 4th German Panzer Armies heading south like a gigantic claw, descending on the oil wells, then to meet with the Axis forces heading toward the Suez Canal.

Three weeks later we were back in the desert for refit and to count the cost of lost equipment and clothing. To my surprise the Quarter Master wanted to charge the lads for items of clothing lost. This had to be taken up with the commanding officer of the unit to stop the QM deducting this charge from their pay.

Mr Churchill once said, to great public applause: 'Give us the tools and we will do the job'. They were words that rang in the ears of the nation. Here in the desert, facing an enemy rampant in victory and ready to deliver the *coup de grâce* was another slogan emblazoned across the side of a truck in the

28

camp of the Royal Engineers next to us: 'Give us the tools and we will pay for them'. They too were having the same trouble as we were, only more so.

At that time, early in August we were encamped in the vicinity of the road out of Cairo along which, we had been informed, Mr Churchill would be passing on his tour of the desert army and all personnel were expected to line the route. Few lined this stretch, though I noticed the truck bearing the message about tools was parked where the Prime Minister couldn't help but see it. This was no politician's pitch; there were no cheering crowds, only disgruntled soldiers that had had a gut full of being pushed around, and were making a silent protest.

Whether this display had any bearing on what happened next I do not know, but changes at the top did take place. The *Crusader* reported changes in the command structure. Bernard Law Montgomery was appointed the new man in charge and soon established himself as a no-nonsense commander ready to meet the ordinary soldier. To them he became known as Monty.

At the end of August a very stirring message was sent from Monty to every soldier, telling us an attack was imminent, to stand fast and to kill the enemy. It was good stuff. I felt part of a team belonging to a body with a purpose. The attack started late one afternoon, with the first shells falling near our armoured command vehicle (ACV), which was manned by members of my troop and from where the divisional commander directed operations. The ACV took off, its lean-to type tents flapping as it disappeared like a gigantic bat out of hell, all seventeen tons of it, into a dip followed by all our radio vans. I remained with my pickup and four men to retrieve what had been left behind and set fire to all stocks of petrol in the area.

Petrol came in four-gallon cans, which were usually stored half-buried in the sand. We set them on fire by stabbing one with a bayonet and throwing in a match, which set off a fire with billowing black smoke. By the time 15 or so small dumps were burning, we must have given the impression to the enemy of a succession of hits.

By the time we had pulled out, an intense exchange of fire had taken place that slowed down the initial strike, and as we moved off trying to follow in the tracks of our troop vehicles, it was getting dark. We were not travelling in open desert but through gullies where vegetation grew abundantly. Shelling from both sides continued with bursts of rifle fire. I had acquired a Bren gun and mounted it on top of my pickup. A few bursts in the direction of the enemy would, I hoped, keep them at a respectful distance.

Around two in the morning we stopped on an incline, taking turns to nap. Lying on my back looking up into a star-studded sky, I could see the shells passing overhead. We were probably in the safest place beneath the flight path of an artillery duel. The shooting stopped at first light, I guessed because of the devastating Air Force raids each dawn.

I took no chances as we moved on, and for the first time in Egypt we ran into a layer of thick fog, and cautiously moved through its thinning layer as the sun appeared above the horizon. In the morning gloom at the crest of a hill, to my surprise we spotted the ACV. Cluttered around it like chicks round a mother hen were the troop's radio vans presenting a perfect target for destruction by marauding enemy aircraft on a raid.

After spreading out, we settled down for the morning brew. Our lieutenant came visiting and asked if we had succeeded in burning the petrol. Just then a plane appeared overhead, it was the 'Lone Ranger'. He came most mornings about one hour after sun-up; brewing-up time, smoke from the fires told him all he wanted to know. With the Bren Gun on my thigh I fired a burst, aiming just ahead, just like pheasant shooting, only this one was way out of range, but we all watched the tracer bullets as they went up. The 'Lone Ranger' turned to go back. Three other planes came in from the west, we scattered, assuming them to be the enemy; one of the three peeled off and shot the ranger down. I felt a little sad, we all knew what he had come for, but he never dropped a bomb or fired a shot. The black smoke poured out as the plane headed down to explode when it hit the ground. A column of smoke marked the spot.

It was nice to share a brew with our Lieutenant. He had really come to discuss the way rations were distributed to the troop. This was becoming an irritant. Daily rations came up in bulk, and it was then my job to see each man got his fair share. Spread out as we were, each crew of each vehicle carried three or four men, and one vehicle with eleven men cooked for themselves. When large tins of fruit, preserves, etc. came up for seven, ten or fifteen men, problems did arise as the contents had to be shared. Vehicles were at least 200 yards apart. It was a thankless job. The Lieutenant ate in the officers' dining tent accompanied by a cook and kitchen equipment. I expressed my opinion that it was time the planners realized this was a modern war on wheels.

There was no other source of food, but good news travels fast – news reached me of the presence of a NAAFI (the army's general store) somewhere ten to twenty miles back. I couldn't go but had to find a like-minded NCO to risk leaving the unit, pooling about £50 to buy mostly beer, chocolate and other goodies he thought fit. It was risky; going absent at a time like this would be classed as desertion in the face of the enemy. Without any doubt a court-martialling offence.

Sweating cobs the next day, anxious for the corporal's return, I sighed with relief when the truck turned up. He went from crew to crew handing out the equivalent of what they put in the kitty, with one restriction: only two bottles of beer per man.

Two days later a Major and a Captain called on me asking for whisky. The second attempt at the same stunt was too close for comfort. As the truck came in the flags went up to move out. We took up a position called 'Lancaster Box', surrounded by minefields, and I stationed my pickup about fifty yards from a single strand of barbed wire marking the boundary. The sun had just set, and a jeep went by. I called out 'stop' but there was no response.

Running after it I saw the jeep go under the barbed wire,

catching the driver across the neck and almost pulling him out. The jeep stopped. When I got there, the driver (an officer) just sat with his head lolling on his shoulder. Fortunately his neck was only partly severed, and he was still breathing. His unit was notified, and within minutes he was taken away. Ironically, a Captain coming to join our signals unit also ran into a minefield, severely damaging both legs. For both these men the war was over.

From these accidents precautions followed: two sand bags were put under the legs of front-seat occupants; at each successive stop all NCO's were to locate minefield boundaries and inform their crews.

This part of the desert was getting crowded. I noticed fresh pink faces, men who had been flown out from England. Also the latest American battle tanks came past our HQ, named Grants and Shermans, they were bigger with greater fire power than those in current use. Chatting with the crews we found they were really pleased with what they had, not because they could match the enemy tanks, but because they could match the 88mm mobile guns that did so much damage.

Morale had certainly been given a boost, and the future looked brighter. Monty was always in the limelight telling the world what he was going to do, and this was heartening. Other positive signs, such as kitbags with unwanted gear being collected, and an extra five days rations of food and water being distributed, indicated that something big was about to happen.

*

On 23 October our sergeant-major, doing the rounds, told us to congregate near our ACV for an important briefing at 10.30 a.m. Monty wasn't there but his staff officers were, with a large scale map of the area highlighting the position of the 10th Armoured Division in a battle line stretching from the Mediterranean to Qatara, a point 30 miles south, where the land fell away, creating a depression of intense heat.

There were no houses, streets or civilians, just a vast sea of

32

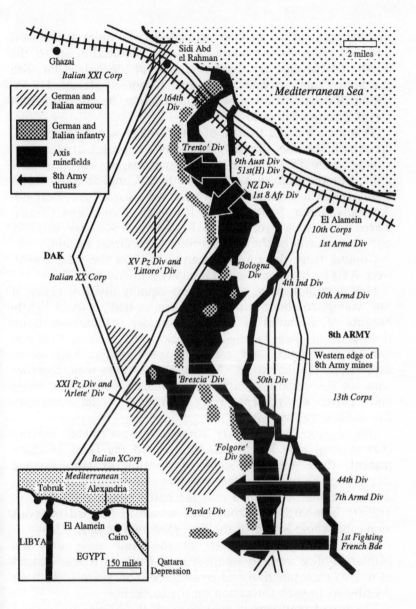

The line-up before the Battle of El Alamein

33

undulating sand we all knew extended 1,500 miles to the west and 500 miles to the south, with the Mediterranean to the north. To the east lay the fertile land of the Nile delta with the Suez Canal beyond. The name 'Alamein' stemmed from the small coastal trading post of that name, on the road from Egypt through Libya to Tunisia.

This then was the theatre of war through which ran a 'thin, crooked black line' that divided the two opposing armies.

Who were they? None were Egyptians, it was not their fight. For the sake of keeping the Suez Canal free for world trade, the Allied forces facing west were from New Zealand, Australia, India, South Africa, Rhodesia, Kenya and Ghana. There was also a Free French Brigade and a Greek Brigade, but the majority of the soldiers were from Great Britain.

Coming from the East, preparing to seize the Suez Canal, were Axis forces from Italy, Germany and Austria.

Half a million men, more or less equally divided, ready, if not willing, to shoot it out. Both armies had to tread lightly because of the miles of deadly landmines – thousands upon thousands of them planted just below the surface. Miles of barbed wire fenced off tracks, boxes, pockets and cages; expressions familiar to us. Among all this were men, together with an assortment of armoured vehicles, soft-skin vehicles and guns, at present lying dormant under whatever camouflage was available.

Our division, and all other formations, were to start moving that evening at 9.30 p.m. Looking round the faces of those present, there were no signs of emotion as they listened intently to the matter-of-fact statement of Monty's intentions. The spokesman continued that the battle would start with an artillery bombardment from guns spaced at 50-yard intervals along the whole length of the line. (*See map on page 33.*)

Mine clearing would start at the same time, and the Military Police were to signpost each track as it was cleared as well as each junction and cross track. The 'plans', had been distributed to each formation on the battle line.

The broad plan was in two parts. Plan 'A' was to try and push through the enemy defences in three days. If that failed, plan 'B' would come into effect and take twelve days, during which time the enemy would be pounded from land, sea and air. With the words 'Good luck', the staff officers collected their bags and map cases and scrambled up the slight incline to their staff car.

Before dispersing the audience was handed over to a chaplain who conducted a short service and blessed us all, though God was far from our immediate thoughts.

Pending action involuntarily quickened the flow of blood through my body as our crew of five chatted over the midday brew about our chances of survival. We finally based our conclusion on calculations drawn in the sand, that, in the next twelve days there would be twenty thousand dead or wounded. Taking into account that we were not exactly in the front line, the odds seemed fairly good at over a hundred to one. We had been shot at, shelled, bombed and strafed by machine-gun fire from the air at intervals during the last three months, and this was going to be a welcome change.

I spent all afternoon checking that each vehicle held five days rations of food and water. In addition, just in case we drifted apart, a further three days' rations were included to tide them over the initial stages of the battle. Doing this was quite exciting for all of us, as if going on a new adventure, and each crew pitched in, making sure their petrol, oil, radiators and tyre pressures were all up to scratch.

Each crew had learned to cook on sand-soaked petrol fires. Each crew had its own water filter made out of empty petrol cans, one half-filled with stones and sand with holes in its base placed on top of an empty can. Every drop of waste liquid from our gallon-a-day ration was tipped into the filter – even urine when recycled made a fair uncorosive mix to keep the radiators topped up.

Just before dusk all units began to move toward starting positions. Dead on 9.30 p.m. the guns opened up. A continuous line of flame along the enemy front did not diminish; as one shell exploded and began to die another took its place and so it continued for 30 minutes. All the while a mass of vehicles moved across the desert under a brilliant moon. I couldn't help remarking to the driver: 'Cocky, I'm glad we're not on the receiving end of this lot'. Standing on the cab seat with the upper half of my body exposed above the cab roof was like having a grandstand view.

The ground shook. The vibrations went through my body, and it was a relief when the shooting stopped as abruptly as it had started. The signal to spread out and settle down for the night was acknowledged by raising a flag. Slowly the dark shapes of this Armada came to rest in the quiet of the night. Wrapped in my ground sheet I lay down beside the truck with my back to the wind, conscious of the sand that slowly built up, as it always did. It was a comfortable feeling.

The next day started with something we could always count on: the sun without a cloud in the sky. Anyone who felt like it cut a petrol can in half, filled it with sand then poured in petrol, put a dixie on top, lit a match, and had an instant fire to brew tea or heat up a meat ration. Today it was Bully and biscuits, washed down with tea. Each did his individual thing, but all sat round the fire to eat. A thin column of smoke rose upward on the hot air as the desert warmed. It seemed a thousand other crews were doing the same thing. From the west a single plane appeared high on the horizon. Scrambling for our guns we watched the plane approach. Though well out of range a hail of tracer bullets went up to meet it. The rising smoke, the tracer bullets and the array of vehicles gave the observer a clear message: we had arrived. The plane, unscathed, turned and disappeared from view.

Letting off a few rounds at breakfast time always helped. But all that day and the next casualties began to mount, as we had no place to take cover, and sporadic shelling of our position continued. But then, this citizens army, averaging 23 years of age, in six months had learned to live in the desert and hoped to survive by making use of every mound, dip or tuft of vegetation that grew in this forsaken wasteland.

Ironically I was the only one in our troop to be hit. It happened on the second day, and fortunately for me it was a spent piece of shrapnel that struck my right thigh. All it did was to tear my trousers and draw a little blood. A little smear

36

of ointment from my first-aid kit put it right.

Each day it was my job to visit the radio vehicle crews with fresh supplies. There were 21 of them. This gave me an exceptional license to travel among other units of the division, passing gun emplacements piled high with empty shell casings. The gunners, stripped to the waist, were loosing off what seemed like tons of shells each day, to be replenished each night, calling on those signal linesmen who worked through the hours of darkness doing what they had to do, and then returned to their forward base to sleep in trenches covered with corrugated iron sheeting.

Everybody had a job to do, and every man was vulnerable. It was a machine at work, with every cog playing its part. The sales blurb spelled it out – it took 60 men behind the line to keep one man at the front. I suppose that should have made us feel good. Not everyone there had that feeling though.

It was the fourth day. Plan 'A' had obviously failed. I had to hand it to those Italian and German soldiers. They had taken all that we could throw at them, yet each day they managed to sling stuff back and the chances were, in this crowded area, most of the stuff found a target.

During those early nights lying on the sand, odd planes would fly high overhead releasing screamers – bombs with a high-pitched whining mechanism. They could not be seen, only the whining got louder, and the nerves in your guts got more on edge, until relief came with the explosion. No one made inquiries, but sleep and relaxation came easier.

At last HQ units of the division began to move forward along mine-cleared tracks lined by four-gallon empty petrol tins painted black with holes on the facing side in the shape of a 'C', or a boat or top hat. Under each tin was a hurricane lamp. Simple, very effective, guiding lights during the night. These were our highways through the minefields with cross tracks that led to cleared areas where we could spread out during the day. It was a marvellous piece of planning.

A body lay at a junction; no one moved it. His rifle with its bayonet was stuck in the ground, his tin hat on top. This was

37

sacred ground, and got a wide birth.

Two days later two of our lads were killed, their radio vehicle riddled by shrapnel. While hitching it up to tow away, a voice from a nearby armoured vehicle called, 'Hurry up, you're attracting fire'.

'So is everyone else', I shouted back, as Cocky pulled away. Just then a shell hit the ground a few yards in front of our vehicle; it was a dud. We watched the shell bounce its way among the scattered vehicles, but it never hit one. Cocky steered our vehicle towards the beaten track as another shell landed some distance away and exploded. It was a lucky escape but none the less we felt like ducks in a shooting gallery.

On our way back, the lone body had been covered with boulders to become a centre-piece of a roundabout we called, 'The Grave'.

The heat was slowly being taken out of the battle and due to that initial briefing there was a time scale to look forward to. It had been circulated that enemy formations were breaking up and withdrawing. During this lull, many units including our own moved back, away from the battle to a man-made oasis, better described as a place of a thousand taps. It was wonderful to bathe, wash away the sand that managed to get into every crevice of the body, to rid our clothes of the microbic livestock we had lived with for many months, and hang them on miles of washing lines to dry.

No brewing up here. Instead, a field kitchen serving steaks and bread; as much as you could eat. Most just wore shorts that had dried on them, and were out playing with footballs. Time was your own to do as you pleased. With nowhere to go, the drinks tent was crowded as the troop was reunited, chatting and laughing over some recent experience. The canteen closed at seven. No fires were permitted, so all that was left was find a spot to sleep, to dream of love and home.

Few stirred at sunrise. Breakfast was served until noon, and then it was back to resume where we had left off 30 hours ago. Clean fresh and well fed, I felt as if I had been on a weeks' holiday, and was now returning to reality as we took up our position in a column advancing through the last of the minefields. Progress was slow in the dark, as the last of the mines were lifted. We were definitely travelling over previously enemy-held territory and hoped to break through at dawn.

Just before first light the first shots were heard. Contact had been made and shooting increased until all hell broke out. All along the line guns were firing and there was the roar of tanks revving up. By 11 a.m. the last of the tanks were through. As our vehicle passed into the open, we came across one of the largest tanks, partially blocking the outlet. It was probably the lead tank from that morning. It was believed to be one of six called 'Churchills'. Unlike its namesake, who was equipped with a large cigar, this tank had the equivalent of a cigarette for a gun. The body had been hit by every conceivable calibre of ammo. Driving round it to spread out I noticed almost every square inch had been dented. By the base of the gun was a hole some six inches in diameter and this was the reason why it had stopped where it had. It was no match against what had hit it.

The scene, as far as my eyes could see, was of black smoke rising from burning tanks and other vehicles. Even beyond the horizon wisps of smoke told the extent of this encounter. By afternoon the stench of decaying bodies strewn over the hot sand and from those still draped over burning tanks emphasized the ferocity of the battle that morning.

It had taken 12 days to get this far after the first bombardment. The dead and wounded would now be tallied. Someone would do the same for the enemy. Now it was time to brew up and have our first meal of the day. A lance-corporal came for a chat. I had first met him as a new-intake militiaman in July 1939. He came carrying a pair of jackboots, and said he had taken them from a German officer half-buried in the sand. 'Hell, haven't you any bloody respect?' I shouted at him. At that he left.

As we chatted over the brew, watching the progress of clearing, transport was arriving to take away the thousands of bedraggled enemy soldiers that had surrendered. They had done their bit and now were shell-shocked, exhausted and begging for water – something we were unable to give from our meagre ration of a gallon a day.

Call it 'Monty's Machine', but whoever was in the driving seat, continuity of purpose did not give way to sentiment. The flags went up and the pursuit of the enemy continued into the setting sun, to end a terrible day.

Early next day contact was made with units of the German 15th Panzer division, knocking out many of their tanks as the drive continued across the open desert, passing well laid-out areas where graves marked the Italian and German soldiers that had died in their attempt to reach the Suez Canal.

That afternoon a strange sight came into view - a vertical wall of sand some two hundred feet high. As we got closer, it struck me as being similar to a bank of cumulus cloud moving across our path: a sandstorm. The wall was going to hit us broadside on. 'Cocky, quick, into the dip, stop and jump out'. Lying flat on the ground, the wall passed over us. Stones and sharp sand tore at our clothes as it roared over our bodies. In the calm that followed, we got up, a little shaken, and were surprised the truck was still standing. We just climbed aboard thankful for small mercies and drove on.

Some miles from Mersa Matruh, with other vehicles of the troop, we began to pick up enemy stragglers and abandoned weapons and headed for the coast road. There were too many minefields that formed part of the costal town's defences to take chances with short cuts. Once on the tarmac road, we met another desert phenomenon. The skies opened up, the rain came down in buckets, and within minutes the desert was a quagmire, and the drive came to a standstill. A wadi in front of us was in full flood, taking with it a three-ton truck, as if someone had turned off a tap, the wadi emptied, and the desert was dry again.

We were guided to the POW cage and handed over the prisoners and a set of barbers instruments I had taken from a very innocent-looking Italian. Cocky did not like that, and said so. To which I replied, 'Cocky: think of it. You with your throat cut. What would be your last thoughts of me?'

In the direction of the recently deserted enemy camp,

soldiers were having fun with four-wheel drive staff cars, motorbikes and other debris lying around. The fun over, the units took up their positions. Once again our vehicle was near the wire, as we called at each vehicle. Most were on the last of their reserve rations. Then we collected all the weapons picked up on the drive, and burned them.

My attention was drawn to a staff car speeding across the minefield, trailed by a cloud of dust. I raised my glasses in time to witness the explosion. Most mines were designed to produce an upward blast. When this one exploded an object that could have been the steering wheel column (or a leg) went straight up, ten feet or more. From the nearest side to me a person scrambled out, 'bare arsed' and naked from the waist to his boots. His shirt hung in shreds just above the waist. His behaviour was erratic as he ran round the vehicle, stopping as if to excrete, then running on. He did several circuits, squatting then running, and finally he just gave up, lowering himself gently to the ground and lying back.

The event must have been seen by others, as an ambulance turned up, one man walking in the staff car's track, guiding the ambulance to do the same. Of the two staff car occupants, the one able to walk was helped, and the other was carried in a blanket into the ambulance that backed out, this time in its own tracks.

A few days went by, and it became clear we were no longer required. The main body were now in Libya, several hundred miles away. From the BBC the bells were ringing in England; Britain was celebrating its first military victory, and Monty was the hero of the hour.

In Russia the battle of Stalingrad was raging. Units no longer required by Monty returned to where they had started. We passed over the same ground at Alamein where the battle was fought a month earlier. It was empty now except for small trucks. Through my field glasses I followed one. It stopped on the side of a hill where it was met by a priest fully dressed for the occasion (though sandblown) and a young blond-haired soldier stripped to the waist carrying a stretcher, who put the tail board down. With the help of the driver,

41

they removed a body wrapped in what looked like sackcloth, and carried it to a prepared grave where the priest said a prayer. Then returned to fetch another body. It was about 10 December, give or take a day, and I wondered what became of the lone soldier whose body, even in death, served in the cause of battle. Was anything left of him? Was his only identity, a dog tag, found lying in the sand? I will never know.

History tells us that during those twelve days, 13,000 Allied soldiers were killed, 8,000 Italians and 1,500 Germans. General Rommel summed it up when he wrote: 'Rivers of blood poured out over miserable strips of land that not even the poorest Arab would have bothered about'. Sergeant major Buonocore of the Italian *Folgere* (paratroop regiment) said of the last day 'For us there was no hope, but the English, too, suffered heavy losses. At one go I counted their burning tanks; there were twenty-one and I fired; I fired; I fired. But they still made a path through the minefield and were upon us. Later that morning, I was a prisoner and the desert a carpet of corpses'.

Leaving that pitiful sight behind us the search for bodies continued, our group moved on to Mena Cap almost in the shadows of the pyramids, the gravestones of the ancient Egyptians. These I had to take a closer look at. The number of tents had grown as more units moved in. The buzz went round we were destined for the northern front.

The opportunity to leave the camp came when transport was laid on at regular intervals to and from Cairo, stopping to pick up or let off those who wished to view the pyramids. On this day I hired a horse as I really wanted to be alone. Cheops, skinned of its alabaster coating to line the Blue Mosque, was crawling with men in uniform, to its very top. One who had made it to the top had met an Egyptian selling cold drinks at double the norm. Two WRNS riding camels led by an Arab added colour. They had come up from the Navy base, near Alexandria. The sphinx had sand bags under its chin; no one expected the enemy to bomb the pyramids or this colossus, so why put them there? The reason given – the middle east was crawling with spies and intelligence units, and

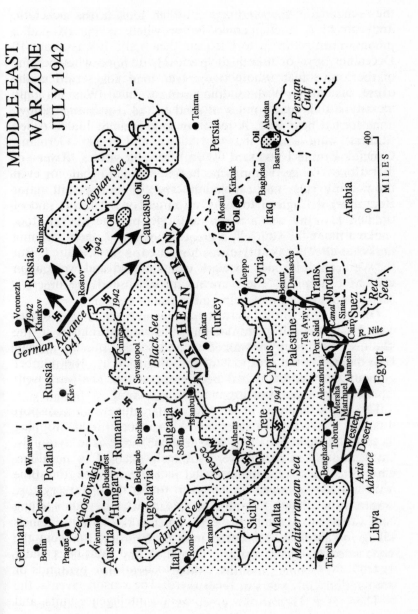

MIDDLE EAST
WAR ZONE
JULY 1942

by re-arranging the sandbags or other items in the area from time to time, a clue could be provided to the date of a photograph.

Going beyond the third pyramid, I noticed strands of barbed wire that usually indicated mine fields, and stayed there, just sitting in the saddle gazing westward with thoughts spanning a thousand miles of sand to the continuing struggle that started near here. A mere ten mile straight run to Cairo. Rommel almost made it.

One morning I was sent for and introduced to a Major and left alone. To my surprise he began by offering me freedom from army rules and regulations and, of course Bull (army discipline) if I agreed to work in Yugoslavia. He was no real soldier, his rank was a token rank. His patter was: 'You can make a name for yourself, a great opportunity', etc.

'What else?' I asked. He was honest enough to say,

'We need radio men to work with the partisans.' I listened, and he continued: 'There are no medals, no recognition and the government cannot help you if you're caught'.

'In that case you will have to double my pay,' I said, half in jest. He would not guarantee that, but would do his best. For the next half hour we walked to and fro in front of the HQ tent discussing the prospects of this Yugoslav involvement.

Four years earlier I had been employed as a private radio operator to a political agent in Orissa, an East Indian state ruled by a number of Rajahs under direct control from London. He was a replacement, his predecessor having been brutally murdered. It was a lonely job, with a price on my head, and where people were strangely affected. A man with tiny arms, that were manipulated in the normal way. Others with grossly enlarged limbs said to be Elephantiasis and where, in a village, I came face to face with a man, his face half eaten away, round the eyes, mucus; like beads of sweat, clung to raw flush. I believed it to be Leprosy. For myself, I contracted malignant malaria almost ending my life. The job lasted over nine months, there were no medals, no recognition, only years of relapses.

Then, as a 21-year-old, green as a cabbage, I managed to

come out of that lot in one piece. Had some ferret in records sent this Major to hunt me down or were my unit getting rid of me? I made no commitments but knew we would meet again.

During the few days break, between leaving the western desert and heading for the northern front, visiting Cairo one could not help noticing groups of soldiers clustered round shopfront windows. I recall visiting all three, from them you learned what was going on round the world. I termed them 'windows of interest'.

3

1943: Through the Holy Land

Leaving the camp near the pyramids we crossed the Nile into Egypt's eastern desert and headed for the Suez Canal where a mass of military hardware and human handlers were spread out on the Sinai desert near Ismailia. Our contingent, via a pontoon bridge spanning the Canal, joined the gathering destined for Aleppo in Syria. This was part of the northern front which had been threatened, though the German forces at this moment were having a hard time.

With the appearance of American and Russian forces in the Middle East, each had its own shop window of interest on the streets of Cairo. Russia displayed pictures of the fighting in Stalingrad, while America showed its troops in Algeria, and the British their own 8th Army, heading toward Tunisia. All three were popular centres for up-to-the-minute information giving a wide perspective and better understanding of the issues facing Europe, Russia, Asia, Africa and the Far East. We were leaving the land of the Egyptians more enlightened than ever before.

On 2 January 1943 the gathering unwound in a snake-like fashion onto a single tarmac strip which crossed the Sinai desert following the ancient trade route from Africa to Be'er Sheva (Beersheba), which has a long and varied history going back to Genesis, situated as it was in the southern region of Palestine on the edge of the Sinai desert (once known as the wilderness).

Entering Beersheba was a unique experience. Through its narrow streets the battle convoy went, stirring up the dust with no outward signs of joy or hate from the tall, unshaven, poker-faced men sitting in groups in the shade of leafy trees, passing round their communal tobacco pipe, and completely ignoring what was going on. The scene, down to the clothes they wore, took most of us back to school days and beyond. It was easy to visualize the teenage Jesus sitting among groups of elders like these, discussing a new creed with aspirations of human brotherhood as opposed to life under the existing establishment. The scenes were as real as those when Christ was a boy. Even the faces resembled the face of Christ as many of those schoolday pictures portrayed Him. He was one of them but had a mind of his own.

We passed on into the land of milk, honey and orange groves. Here, in contrast, we were met by boisterous gangs of teenagers employed to harvest the oranges. They *pelted* us with oranges! Whether in hate or fun or a bit of both, the youthful laughter from both sides made it more like a 'bun fight'. One thing was certain, we welcomed any oranges which landed in our vehicle.

Oranges were piled in set quantities along the side of the road ready to be collected, and it was a wonderful sight. Most would have been willing to stop and buy but for the urgency of the convoy to keep moving. Those that landed in our vehicle were welcome fruits as many of us were suffering from desert sores. The remedy in Egypt's western desert was ascorbic tablets, each said to contain vitamin C equal to that of four lemons. They appeared to have no effect as a remedy. From these sores ran a clear liquid, and only bandages gave some relief, but bandages were hard to come by.

It cleared up after two or three days in Syria's cooler climate and eating fresh vegetables. If the condition had a name, I never knew it. We camped just outside Gaza within easy reach of the town where food, drink, night life and brothels made it quite a town to stop by. The midnight call for help from the madams of the overworked establishments brought out the military police, who were an essential part of our convoy.

The next day we travelled through what can only be described as the cradle of Christianity, with roads signs to Jerusalem, Samaria, and Nazareth, that kept my mind riveted

47

to the Bible. I thought of Salome, her father Herod, and the unfortunate John the Baptist who heralded the coming of a new Messiah. His head ended up on a plate, as a gift to Salome for doing what can only be described as a provocative cabaret in front of a bunch of Herod's lecherous friends.

Then a large sign came into view with a blue band inscribed 'Sea Level' and there, 686 feet below was the Sea of Galilee (or Sea of Tiberias). No fishermen were throwing out their nets, no boats were trawling, no one was walking on its waters; there was only an alien army on wheels in a continuous column wending its way down and along the sea's 14 mile length to climb the ascending road on the far side. As we reached the bottom, the flags went up, signalling a halt to brew up.

Whatever the consequences, we couldn't resist running 'starkers' into that Biblical water before continuing on to Damascus, to camp for the night. It was there, out on a spree, I first tasted 'Van der Hum', a South African liquor that has been one of my favoured drinks ever since.

On the fourth day the convoy reached Aleppo where units were directed onto roads leading to predetermined camping sites. Our unit ascended a rock-strewn hill to the west of the city within easy reach of the city centre where military police were always in evidence.

The area was captured by the British in 1918, and then mandated to France by the League of nations. In 1941, and the surrender of France to Germany, Syria became an independent republic. The Free French government recognized the independence, but due to the instability of the area, the French backed by Britain continued to occupy the country. Aleppo was a city of some 300,000 inhabitants; Arabs; Moslems; Jews; Christians; Armenians; Turks and other factions lived in harmony under a French civil authority. From general discussions at meetings it became clear our presence, ostensibly, to defend the Suez Canal, had turned into a mission to keep the peace in the presence of the German withdrawal from the Caucasus, and to hold the existing national borders. This was manifested by the

48

occasional show of strength, parading military hardware through the streets. There was an airport about two miles west of the city that had recently been used by German aircrews. Their air staff had lived in the Baron Hotel in the heart of the city. It would not have mattered to the population what nation the occupying battalions represented, so long as they brought with them salvation. It appeared the whole area from the Suez to the Turkish border had never known freedom to rule as sovereign states.

Aleppo was a sophisticated, cosmopolitan city serving good food, with a variety of shops, restaurants, and a cinema currently showing 'Quelque dans Les Rocky'. French was the language of the street. Female company was to be found in the nights spots and cabarets that varied with the cultures of the resident population. Moslem girls ventured on the streets during the day, despite the strict code of conduct placed on them, the young and the pretty ones wore the thinnest veils through which the whites of their eyes flashed, and their teeth enhanced the beauty of their friendly smiling faces. The feminine magic and mystique was all there; but not for sampling.

A communication centre was established in a municipal building opposite the French state Major's residence, to which I was assigned as Superintendent, and discovered the composition of this force that included the Arab legion, Greeks, Indians, French and British. Morse code was used extensively to communicate and it was good to get on the international waves again and listen to the different nationals together with the renowned Baghdad style of Morse, that came as music to my ears. Each school of telegraphists across the world had their own style of putting together dots and dashes, like a dialect in the dot-dash language.

To keep abreast of the activities of the German 1st and 4th panzer armies that were in the process of withdrawing from the Caucasus, due to Russian successes at Stalingrad, the military put on the latest newsreels from that battlefront at the local cinema. By the end of January this most brutal battle had ended, and I was grateful that the lads who came

49

to Egypt in the *Nea Hellas* had been spared involvement on the northern front.

History tells us that the 250,000-strong 6th German army, in their battle for Stalingrad, lost 90 per cent of their soldiers. They were killed in action, or died in captivity, or froze to death. All were buried in mass graves. Almost a million Russian soldiers and civilians died as well, to save their homeland from occupation. Film showed that those last days were fought in conditions that made Alamein seem like a tea party. General Doerr of the German High Command, summed it up: 'For every house, workshop, water tower, railway embankment, wall, cellar and pile of rubble, a bitter battle was waged. The distance between the enemy's army and ours was as small as it could possibly be.'

The lull that usually sets in after danger has passed brought with it inertia – a fatal disease that only involvement with the population could cure, and so the military turned its attention to football.

Aleppo possessed a good football pitch and matches were well attended. We became involved, mixing and socializing with the locals and helping to swell the number of spectators, even getting ourselves in the local newspaper. The army at last woke up and invited a professional UK team to play a regional team; that filled the stadium. With the Syrian economy down to using cinema tickets for small change, it was the presence of the army that helped keep a stable economic, social and political balance.

Then came the head-hunters, a travelling circus of junior officers whose task it was to seek out volunteers, usually for the more hazardous tours of duty, or those conjured up by the dirty tricks brigade. The very presence of the hunters was a clear sign that units on this front were about to break up. What astonished me were the sheer number of soldiers ready to put themselves forward for parachute regiments, for covert operations and any other un-military activity on offer. There were some ten tables where interviews were taking place, with a crowd sitting in the sun outside awaiting their turn.

With spring in the air and little to do, Beirut became the

outlet for ten day holiday periods spread out over March, April and May. By this time all enemy forces had been driven out of north Africa and the German forces on the Russian front were retreating into the Ukraine. Hitler's dream of conquest had been shattered.

My only attempt to catch up with history in this area was to visit the tomb of Zacharias, said to be the father of John the Baptist, situated near the mosque of Zachariah. In June, I received notice to report to the parachute training battalion at Haifa in Palestine and, surprisingly I was the only one from our unit. At Aleppo station I met a group dressed in identical civilian clothes. They were British, stuck out like sore thumbs, and were heading for Turkey. Although Turkey was a neutral country and any threat from Germany now non-existent, I wondered where they would turn up.

*

On the Monday of the second week of June 1943, 32 men, all strangers, from many different regiments and stations in the Middle East, assembled to meet their mentors for the next four weeks. The parachute training battalion was situated at a place called Ramat David, some 15 miles east of Haifa and Mt Carmel, among vineyards and corn fields, with scattered settlements, known as communes, housing Jewish refugees from Europe (the lucky ones). A mile to the south was a small aerodrome, to the north a dropping zone that was in full view of our barracks, as well as the public. Each morning between 5 and 7 a.m. the spectacle of streams of bodies tumbling from planes was a must for the viewing public. The old sweats, around 23 years of age, having got their wings, kept up a running commentary on what our immediate future held in store for us.

At 9 a.m. sharp the chief instructor explained our training programme. We were to be divided into groups of eight, known as sticks, each with a leader. The leader would be responsible to see that his stick arrived at the training ground, at 9 a.m. Among the group were one Lieutenant, two

51

sergeants and one corporal, and the rest fell in to make up the four sticks. Off we went at the double. The path led through fields of ripening corn – never had I seen a wheat crop quite like this, stalks standing straight, four feet high with heads of wheat six inches in length. We never grew wheat like this on the farms in Sussex. This land of Canaan really was a land of plenty.

Among the group were four Irishmen, the heart and soul of each mornings' journey to the training ground, they whistled Irish jigs all the way.

The training was based on team work, understanding of each others' faults and capabilities, and how best to mould each to make a winning team. The training ground was about one acre in size, with an open-ended hanger that provided the only shade on this sunbaked pad, on which we were subjected to four periods of gruelling exercises.

The grub trolley would arrive about 11 a.m., laden with doorstep sandwiches, but no tea. If you wanted liquid – and we all did – it was to be found in the fire buckets along the hanger wall. Each day there would be a rush for the buckets to replace the sweat that had oozed from our bodies. All this was watched by the fire tender crew who showed a minimal interest as they waited to refill the buckets – they had seen it all before. Then came the physical stuff – pitting strength against each other, singly, in pairs, in fours then stick against stick followed by a general scrummage with a Rugby ball. None of us were macho types, just average Joes of different shapes and sizes from many walks of life enjoying ourselves.

It was surprising how happy I felt on that mile-long double back to barracks, the excited chatter through the midday meal. The afternoons were spent on Haifa's beach to take in salt lost in the mornings sweat. The care taken of our well being, after three years of war, was pronounced in this training. Two-and-a-half hours swimming, surfing and chatting up the girls that happened to be there as well. So it went on each day during the first week. I cannot recall one incident of foul play.

On Monday morning of the second week, three from the

group were missing, thankfully none from my Stick. No explanation was given and questions on the subject were not answered. I got the feeling we were under careful scrutiny from morning to night. The week went on with bone-crushing exercises, like jumping from moving objects, dropping from high towers in a safety harness, followed by competitive team games, not forgetting the telegraph pole each stick threw high in the air to catch as it came down.

We looked forward to the afternoons on the beach and were learning how to relax. Unfortunately, Fatty Simms, of my stick, broke his leg. Within minutes he was whisked away by an RAF ambulance. I made inquiries at the battalion office later in the day but the office wallah, like most, was reluctant to give me any information. Pulling out all the stops I said, 'He is from my stick, from the same regiment, and I am the senior NCO of that regiment at this battalion. Where was he taken?'

'To a hospital in Nazareth' he grudgingly replied.

On Monday of the third week only 26 assembled at the training ground. We had got the message – no questions. Five had disappeared without a trace, without any reasons given, not even a goodbye. The day was taken up with the parachute: how it was constructed; tear strength of the material; the number of cords and their break strength. This confidence-building knowledge was followed by folding and packing. The 'chute's canopy, when opened, had a diameter of 28 feet, with a 60-foot stretch when laid out from harness to apex strap. The vital link was a small cord with just 200 pounds break strength. This was tied, strictly in a reef knot, at the point where all the cords crossed at the apex of the canopy, then to a strap, and the free end dangled from the top of the 'chute's pack that would be clipped to another strap fixed to the plane, and was known as the static line, thus giving the sensation of free-falling some 80 feet before the 'chute's canopy opened.

The whole group practised dummy runs from a spare aircraft, an 'Anson' that took up to ten men with an exit door about 5 feet high with little room to spare in width. A person called the dispatcher was there to make sure we knew the drill. In the process he stressed the need for each man to clip the free end of the strap attached his parachute to the aircraft's fixed line, and never let it out of their grasp until they reached the door. He added, 'You never know who is behind you'. We thought that funny and laughed but he was serious.

At 5 a.m. on Tuesday morning we assembled at the airport. There were only three sticks. We were to jump in pairs; the Lieutenants' stick boarded the first plane, my stick the second and ten men boarded the third. Leaders were expected to be first to try out every exercise, and now were first to jump. As our aircraft approached the dropping zone a red light came on. The first pair, with me as no. 1, stood by the open door looking down into 2,000 feet of nothing and feeling really scared. Then the green light came on.

Forgetting everything I had been taught, I put my right foot out, as if to test the air, and was caught by the slipstream (the wind from the propellers), which spun me round to crash into the door frame. I vaguely remember the dispatcher's push that sent me sliding spreadeagled along the fuselage. I must have blacked out for a second or two but came to sitting in my harness floating in pure silence blissfully unaware of my surroundings. Reality returned with the voice of an instructor on the ground saying, 'Knees and feet together, that's it'. Looking down in horror, I saw the ground coming up to meet me. Panic was taking over when the soothing voice continued, 'Keep those feet together, knees slightly bent, that's good. Well done'. Those last two words reached me as I lay half stunned on my back wondering what the hell had happened. 'Release your parachute, roll it up and take it with you to the truck'. Realizing I was still in one piece, looked for my no. 2. No one else was on the ground and I asked, 'Where is number 2?'

'You were the only one.'

The plane came round again, and I asked the first to land, 'What happened to Joe?' He looked at me in surprise.

'Christ, I thought you were a gonna. You frightened Joe.

He refused to jump after what happened to you.'

We had another jump to do, and on the way back to the airport I felt a little guilty. Joe was not at the airport. I never saw him again. Seven of us left the truck, picked up fresh parachutes and boarded the plane. We were to jump in the same order. The dispatcher said, good humouredly, 'No. 1, do you think you could make a better exit this time?' Some chuckled as we connected our 'chutes to the static lines, and sat down to wait for take off.

This time the dispatcher stood near, his hand on my pack, and when the light turned green eased me forward into free-fall. I saw my 'chute being pulled out, I felt the jerk as the vital 200 pound cord snapped and watched the canopy open to experience once again the rare silence while sitting in my harness. Then the voice from below: 'Good, keep that position, you are on your own'. Looking down, I felt no panic this time, and concentrated on calculating when to give the final pull on the cords to break the force of impact about a foot from the ground. It worked like a charm.

Then near tragedy struck with the third pair. As we watched, someone was still attached to the plane and was being trailed along, his legs tangled in the static lines. 'Its the man of method!' one shouted.

Yes, it was Ole Bill, my private name for William Gilchrist who slept two beds away from me. His routine never varied.

The dispatcher had managed to pull him in by the time the plane came round again to drop the last pair. To our surprise three came out. 'It's Half Pint! God that mans got guts!' We rushed to greet him and help him up. 'You deserve a drink, Half Pint,' said Charlie Vogue, who always referred to Bill as Half Pint. Sometimes Half Pint Jesus. The name derived from the interpretation of 'Gill Christ': half pint Jesus. Any mishap of this kind provoked lively banter as we returned to barracks. In the showers the outline of the harness showed up as bruises on Half Pint.

During the morning a group of 'trick cyclists' put us through some psycho tests; no one took them seriously but we played along with them. Then we had a talk on the Pacific war – the American army's victory in February at Guadalcanal and their continuing successes over the Japanese. This was followed by yet another talk on the intentions and role of the Special Forces in Europe, code-named 'EO' (executive operations). This ranged from assassinations, destruction of strategic installations, information-gathering and radiomen operating behind the enemy lines. This talk was directed at us as a foretaste of things to come.

The rest of the day was our own, and with a few others, we decided to explore the city if Haifa, situated at the north-east corner of Palestine. There were warships anchored in the Bay of Acre, and a few military personnel like us, just visiting or on holiday. We strolled up Mount Carmel, which could easily be recognized as 'nob hill', where rich and more affluent members of the community lived. Beirut had its 'nob hill' too, called the Cedars.

From Haifa's railway station ran a line to Suez in Egypt, a new line to Turkey, and another to Damascus and Jordan. It also had a smart bus depot, for this was a growing city attracting immigrant Jews from its catchment area. Its waterfront certainly had a future. We dined in a street-side café, and no police were in evidence, only naval shore patrols, in parties of six to eight, that dealt with any rowdiness. The military were careful to avoid civil confrontation.

It had been a long day, and we finally returned to camp at Ramat David. I called in to the sergeants' mess for a drink before turning in, so it was late when I got to my bed, and all in the room were prone, except Bill, 'the man of method'. He hadn't quite finished laying out his kit as I bade him goodnight'.

But what a night it turned out to be, tossing and turning with one nightmare after another, dreaming of attempts to land behind enemy lines. There were Roman candles (chutes not opening), crash landings, bullets busting through the fuselage and tearing holes in my parachute. Never had I welcomed a dawn so much as this one, as the morning light slowly lit up the barrack room to dispel the torments of the night. I felt limp and exhausted as the group assembled for

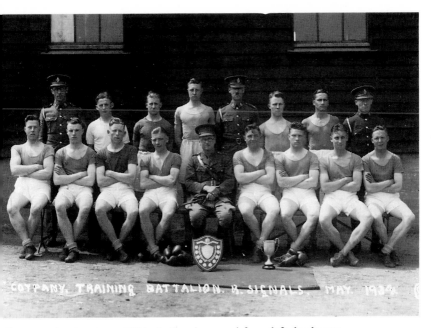

Company boxing team, 1934. Author is second from left, back row

ootball match, Aleppo 1943. Author is second from left, second row

Armoured car of the Guards' Brigade, Aleppo 1943

Armoured Command Vehicles used by 10th Armoured Division Signals in the Western Desert, Aleppo 1943

The Author wine tasting, Accra, West Africa, 1952

Time off in Southampton. The author with his wife and family, c.1953

Baling hay on the farm, 1970s

Crossbow tournament, 1980s

two more jumps. Bill came out, and approaching me, said: 'I'm not jumping. I'm not afraid. But after last night ... he paused. 'This life is not for me.' I understood, but said nothing, for that was his entitlement. We were all volunteers and as such were free to back out during training.

My stick had been reduced to six. The chief instructor nodded, and said he had two replacements. We were to jump in fours. The two replacements were oldies, one a Colonel, the other a Major, both at least ten years senior and, probably, considered too old to go through the initial groundwork. All they needed was the experience of a few jumps. One became my no. 2 and the other the no. 2 of the second four. It was policy to warn everyone in the stick that aliens were among them, ie. two unknown quantities, and to make sure they went through the door.

All went well and the specials were keen to carry on for the second drop – any future drop for them would be behind enemy lines. We all shook hands and wished each other well before going our separate ways. Somehow, at times like this, rank did not matter. We were all professionals in something, all volunteers sticking our necks out, without any thoughts of King or country. This, above all, was recognized.

For me it was back to bed and real sleep. When I awoke in the late afternoon, there was a large notice on my bed: 'Do not disturb, nightmares'. I was not the only one flat out that day.

All my fears had vanished with four jumps under my belt, and with only 24 men left we were to jump in sticks of eight. The challenge for the best, evenly-spaced descent was on, for the straightest line with a uniform slope in the shortest distance. No matter what, the army always ends up with a passing-out parade, and this was the run-up to ours. It was getting more of a game by the minute as the planes lined up and the dispatchers appeared just as keen to get the act right. Wind conditions were given as gusting. This meant as soon as you hit the ground you had to release your harness or suffer being dragged, lifted and dumped somewhere else. All three sticks came out without incident but not without criticism and

57

went up to try again.

The following day two containers were loaded in the bomb bay that had to be released after the first four had jumped; the leaders were to release them after the fourth man went out. Count one, two, trip the switches and rush for the door. The first round went well. The final tuning by our instructor before going up for the last jump of the course. As fate would have it, tragedy struck. The first two sticks made passable descents and were watching the last stick. They were doing fine until the seventh man dropped like a stone. I could see the free end of his strap as he rolled over and over until he hit the ground to split open like a ripe windfall apple. The markers, referees and instructors rushed forward to prevent us approaching the body. There was an enquiry later that morning, but only those concerned with the training programme attended.

On the following Monday morning 20 men of the 32 who had assembled three weeks earlier received their wings. We were then informed that from today we would be entitled to two shillings per day until further notice. It was no big deal, but we wore our wings with pride. All that week was spent on small arms assault weapons. It became very clear that the .303 Lee Enfield rifle, the weapon that had maintained law and order across a quarter of the earths surface in the name of the British Empire had had its day. In its place came the first of the new breed – the Sten Gun. By comparison, this was a cheap, deadly, close-quarter weapon with the fire power of the Thompsons sub-machine Gun. The gangsters gun.

It had been a gruelling month, much sweat had been lost, but much, very much, human friendship, understanding and comradeship gained. There was no valedictory parade, no final booze-up and there were no goodbyes. By the very nature of the group, it was unlikely we would meet again.

With one more commitment in mind, I set off on Saturday morning with a like-minded person, John Parks, also from the Royal signals, to see Fatty Simms in Nazareth. Our journey took us across a large farming commune with well-kept vineyards, and recently harvested corn fields. We skirted the farmstead, housing a herd of Friesian cows, a combine harvester and other mechanized agricultural tools. It all oozed prosperity and dedication.

No one stopped to question us, and it was the sabbath, but, I sensed, we were being trailed. The British were not popular with either Jew or Arab but were there to maintain peace, law and order. None the less I realized we were trespassing and were causing concern to the management of the commune. On our own farm in Sussex the whole family would become suspicious of any trespasser passing over our land and would be watched until they reached the boundary. As we were due to pass this way the next day, I decided we should enter by the front gate and request permission to cross the vineyard to the camp. We were on dangerous ground, unarmed, without permission to leave the camp and we had not told anyone where we were going. Something that had not been considered.

A mile further on we came across an Arab home with a white-walled enclosure, and stopped by the roadside to brew up. The owner came out. In perfect English asked where we were going and where we had come from. He knew the parachute camp, was sorry to hear about Fatty Simms, and invited us to have a meal at his house on our return. Not far from his home was what must have been the heart of his farm where men sat smoking their hubble bubble pipes while women tossed bundles of unthreshed corn into the path of a donkey that was being coerced round and round by a teenage boy in an attempt to separate the seed from the wheat stalks. The gulf that separated the Arab from the Jew was indeed wide. I could not help but wonder what the future held for this land.

Nazareth came up to expectations looking just as it had in the picture books of my school days, and we had no difficulty in locating the military hospital. Fatty had not expected any visitors but was really pleased to see us. Questions flowed from him but when he asked how many got through sadness clearly showed up and it was his bad luck in dropping out when he did. The sight of our wings brought tears that trickled down his cheek, because he knew he would never be given another chance. His leg was in plaster, and we sat in the canteen all that afternoon and into the night, just chatting – that was all we could do for him. He limped his way to the door to see us out, knowing we would never meet again.

Out in the town, the street empty, we met an Israeli policeman. He warned us that a curfew existed and suggested we sleep in a recess of a municipal building, advising one of us to stay awake. Something was not right – you could feel the tension in the air, and did as we were advised.

We left at first light, brewing up about a mile out of town. It was the last of the petrol from a wine bottle that we poured on the dry soil to heat up two mess tins of water for coffee. The sun came up to warm our chilled bodies as we leisurely munched a chocolate bar, lying on the grassy bank planning our return by map. We had made the outward journey by compass and decided to return by road to arrive at the Arab's house about midday. I wanted to see how the corn was collected and how much. John would take the road and I would retrace my steps over the hill. Much of the way we were in sight of each other. At the heart of the farm there were only women gathering the scrapings from the ground into a sieve where the donkey had walked. Tossing the contents of the sieve into the air allowed the wind to blow away the chaff, and the fine mesh allowed the dust through until all that was left was a handful of seed, and this yield from their meagre crop was carefully tipped into a bag, a process that would last for several days for a 100 kilos of seed. Continuing my journey I sensed I was not alone – someone was following me, and I suddenly stopped to scratch my leg and a figure darted behind a bush to lie flat. I soon discovered it was a young girl. Her cover blown, she ran down the side of the hill. The next time I saw her she was way ahead, hurrying toward the Arab's house.

At the Arab farm house the family greeted us. The man who spoke to us the previous day was not present, and a youth who spoke English said his father had to leave on business. Present were his mother and what I took to be her daughter, who, I suspected was the stalker on the hill. She smiled and walked beside me as mum guided us to the front veranda. There were no chairs, only a mat on which was a large round dish containing a stew-like substance at its centre. Probably nanny goat. Mum and the girl removed their yashmaks, mum indicated for all to be seated, and handed round a flat loaf of bread. John and I waited hoping one of the family would start so we could follow. The young man was eager to learn about our customs and kept the table talk going while everyone broke bread and dipped it in the communal dish, scooping out moderate amounts of goat.

A boy of about ten years old rushed in, and planted himself between John and I, giving me an opportunity to get closer to the girl. The boy spoke a few words to his mother and then looked up at us in turn and smiled, like boys of that age do. Mum passed him some bread and he immediately tucked in to what was going. His legs were covered in sores. I asked the youth how he came to be like that. He just shrugged and said, 'He is always playing in the dirt'. Somehow I felt quite at home and wanted to converse with the girl for there existed a spark of telepathic interest between us. Neither mum, who followed the conversation, nor the youth, appeared willing to ease us over the culture gap.

The dish empty, we lingered, as I did not want to give up on the girl, and asked mum if I could attend to the sores on the boy's legs. She looked surprised, but beckoned the girl to bring water and a towel. I had never used the new first-aid pack sewn into my trousers, and this was an opportunity to find out its contents. The girl brought a box and told the boy to sit on it. She knelt down beside me as we worked on the boy's legs, washing and applying ointment and then loosely bandaging the worst parts. This brought our bodies closer together, our bare arms deliberately making contact. Our eyes met, and there was that unmistakable desire for each other. My lapse of propriety in this encounter must have alerted John for at this point he said, 'It's time we went'. It jolted me back to reality. A little self-conscious I rose from my kneeling position, and the girl quickly collected the bowl and towel and hurried away. There was silence all around. Nodding to mum, I turned to the two boys who were regarding me with a curious look in their eyes, nodded to them, and left with John. Looking back at the gate to wave goodbye, the girl was nowhere to be seen.

'Sod it! I was getting on well there.'

'Too well,' said John. 'Mum was getting worried at you two, I had to break it up.'

Strolling along the road we discussed the complexity of life in a land with so many creeds and cultures. That I had been driven to search out Salomes to satisfy a basic need was interesting, frustrating, wonderful, but shallow. Deep-rooted love seemed impossible.

Arriving at the entrance to the Jewish commune, we knew there were many girls around, though we had been strictly forbidden to fraternize with them. Entering the main gate we were met and invited in for refreshment we did not want, but could not refuse the seemingly genuine hospitality. In general conversation (they all spoke English) we were questioned about our purpose. They also showed an interest in the parachute school, implying that, perhaps, it might now be closed down. There was a general exodus of troops from the Middle East to the Far East and into the European theatre. There was a strong possibility that the training camp would close, and we understood their anxiety, with so many young men and young girls so near each other, something would have to give. Shaking hands on that friendly note the elder led us out to point the way to the camp. It was a working day, the vineyard seemed alive with girls tending the vines, but none appeared to be friendly. They too must have received the same message.

Reporting to the guardroom we discovered we were due for ten days holiday in Tel Aviv, a seaside resort that reminded me of Brighton in Sussex, only with blue skies guaranteed. The hotel was right on the seafront, and the accommodation was paid for by the powers-that-be. We made friends with a Jewish family and socialized with their friends, and that ten days was a wonderful break. Our wings did not go unnoticed by the female population either. Remarks were made in passing like: 'Have you had any jumps lately?'

On the last day, telegrams waited for us. They were identical: 'Report to a signals holding unit at El Minha south of Cairo under your own steam'. It took a couple of days, more or less hitch-hiking via Ghaza and Ismailia to reach our destination. By that time I had contracted severe ear trouble, and ended up in a New Zealand hospital. After three weeks the New Zealand authorities sent me on another three weeks' convalescence in Luxor.

Here all the patients, after showering, were dressed in blue trousers, white shirt and blue jacket. Everything was so casual – it was a place where mind and body could really relax, rank or regiment was never mentioned. On the last day I received my uniform washed and ironed with a pass to board the New Zealand bus back to El Minha camp.

*

Holding camps are places where soldiers are held to fill regimental requirements as required. I found myself with a covey of sergeants and warrant officers with nothing to do. Visits to Cairo were daily, but its streets were no longer bustling with khaki-clad figures. The American and British armies had invaded the island of Sicily with bridgeheads on Italian soil. The windows of interest were now displaying pictures of the advances in Italy and Russia.

I had not been paid for three months. Visiting army HQ in Cairo, I located the pay office, surrendered my pay book to be brought up to date, and to my surprise out came a Captain with a fist full of papers who said: 'Sergeant, I don't know how you've managed it, you haven't paid any income tax since the war began. You owe well over 50 pounds and that is about all the money you have coming to you'. It was hard to believe. In the desert the quarter master was trying to make soldiers pay for tools and items of clothing lost in battle. This Captain, it appeared, believed that all good soldiers should pay like everybody else for the war – if not

63

with their lives, then from monies received if the soldier was fortunate enough to survive. And no doubt he would be willing to delve into the two-bob a day for qualifying as a paratrooper. But four years of war had a mellowing effect and he had his job to do.

'OK, take it, but I would like to speak to you in private.' In his office I told him I needed the money as I was spent out and would be going on a mission that would last for some time. he could *then* take what he wanted. He was no die hard at heart, just a keen follower of King's rules and regulations, a bureaucrat vigorously pursuing the living and the dead for sums due to His Majesties Government. But as I was skint he agreed to sanction a payment of £50 in advance.

It was the end of September when I reported to the Yugoslav Office in the smart area of Cairo and was then taken to a villa kept by a Yugoslav family. John Parks was already installed with a number of Slav personnel, and the only other person who spoke English was a 19-year-old daughter of the family. Parks and I shared a bedroom that overlooked a tree-lined avenue where the daily life of the suburb was on show. The houses were more or less the same as those found in suburban England, owned by office types coming and going each day by car, bicycle and on foot.

Across the street, a young man had died. For the next three days women criers came crying down the street to the house, intermittently breaking out with shrieks of imitation grief.

John left each morning and was away most of the day. Where he went and what he did was never mentioned. Whereas I had received books on the Balkans and its history, leading up to the Balkan entente giving its blessing to a new state, Yugoslavia (young Slavia) with guarantees from neighbouring countries to protect the union. Some books were recommended, some compulsory reading. Then came files containing details of meetings held at Bihăc in Bosnia between the leaders of ethnic groups, followed by maps with notes on weather patterns expected from Montinegro to Slovenia, the Dalmation coast and the Adriatic sea. Swotting all this stuff was interesting and all the while new faces came and old faces went. There was a room wired out for morse sending and receiving. I knew I was being checked out, and was even writing letters for others and reports on various situations given to me in a botched up Serbo-Croat/English mix. At last I was led up to an attic room where a suitcase Trans receiver was installed, and sat in with a Yugoslav who instructed me on the precise procedure used to communicate with agents, wherever they may be holed up.

John Parks had disappeared without so much as a handshake. The daughter, who actually worked for the Inter-Services Liaison Department (ISLD), spoke seven languages. From our conversation I gathered she had been nurtured from childhood, attending various schools in Cairo with English, German, Italian, French as second languages. Evening discussions were conducted by the girl, and in this way I began to pick up Serbo-Croat and realized that these Slavs, who were about my own age, were able to converse with Poles or Russians, as well as with the ethnic groups without much difficulty. My radio log, which I wrote in Serbo-Croat, was scrutinized daily as was every contact for punctuality; this above all was the essence of this network. In December the outfit moved to Italy and settled down in Bari.

4

1944: The Year of my Life – After the Bean Pushers' Ball

1944 is the year I will never forget; it was certainly the most formative. The fortunes of war had changed direction during 1943: for Russia, America and the British. All three groups, with gathering strength, had won decisive battles against Germany, Italy and Japan, who, for the first time since 1939 had been stopped and forced onto the defensive and into retreat.

My role as a troop sergeant in an armoured division had come to an end. I like many others, remained floating in the eddy currents that formed on the edge of a mass migration of khaki-clad souls that streamed from the middle east, destined to take up positions in other parts of the world for the final battles that must come.

Those on the edge found themselves in parachute schools and honing skills necessary for covert operations. Useful though many of these individual skills were, they were side issues that did not really interest me. My real calling was radio, as I was able to communicate with the best through the medium of morse code. For this I took up a comfortable residence in a villa on the outskirts of Cairo, where I did my real work, sending and receiving information, to where and to whom I didn't ask. Messages were always in the originator's personal code and open to interception by anyone in the business. Radio deception and preventative tactics were the mode of the time – to delay, confuse and fragment to prevent or delay decoding. Practices that could only be learned by usage.

My companions were members of Yugoslavia's ethnic groups, with whom I studied their history from the Balkan entente of the late 1920s to the ongoing political strife that was dividing the country in 1943, when it was occupied and under the heel of the German jackboot. Efforts to unify resistance, to share available resources, to cooperate within their own realm were not always acceptable to the luminaries in Yugoslavia at the time. King Peter had gone, and the power vacuum that had resulted was rapidly being filled by men with very different aspirations.

From the Allies' point of view, with all eyes on Europe, it was necessary to maintain strong underground resistance in order to hold down as many German divisions as possible. The Allies' main aim was the success of the second front.

It didn't work. Many Yugoslavs wondered whether it were not the case that the Allies, Britain in particular, were prepared to fight to the last Yugoslav in order to achieve their own ends. All this prepared me for the life I might have to live with, and gave me a sense of purpose. Unfortunately, political shenanigans seldom please everybody. General Mikhailovich, who controlled the Serbians, and Pavelic, leader of the Ustase (Croat insurgents) were at loggerheads. Both these men regarded Josip Broz as a no-good communist. Broz was a trained communist politico out of Moscow gaining national acclaim as a leader and catalyst for change in Yugoslavia. He was known as Tito, and he organized most of the resistance, and because of it received the support of the Allies though we all suspected it was to the Russians he would eventually turn for salvation.

Our group (ISLD) had agents scattered among the now warring factions in Yugoslavia and advised each cell, if serving with the Chetnik Serbs, or with the Ustashi, either give themselves up to the Germans, make contact with Tito's partisans or make for the Adriatic coast in the hope of being picked up by one of the E-boats that operated in the area. They could have added 'And the best of British luck.

This was the background to my arrival in Bari, southern Italy, in December 1943, to see hanging on the office wall a

67

colour portrait of Marshall Tito. Like all the others he had appointed himself to a 'top brass' rank. By January 1944 he was the undisputed leader in Yugoslavia, and until that time most of our agents operated in Bosnia and Serbia.

It was in Bari where I teamed up with two others destined for northern Yugoslavia. The Allied armies were still struggling up the leg of Italy, and where we were intending to operate was virgin territory to the ISLD. Our cell comprised a Captain from the Royal Engineers from Manchester, a sergeant from the Rhodesian army, an ex-gold mine executive from Bulawayo, and myself, a sergeant in the Royal Signals, ex-farm boy, from East Sussex, and the youngest of the group.

We had never met before and knew little more than what each needed to know, which was very little. The operation, code named Volt, had been assigned to us and was due to be launched during the January moon between 16 and 20 January 1944. It got off to a bad start. Three nights on the trot the crew of a Halifax bomber went in search of a dropping zone. Each night we sat round a hole in the floor of the bomber, ready to go. For some reason, probably because of the 'need to know', none questioned why we were free winging over enemy territory while they, the enemy, were using us for target practice.

Privately, I had some misgivings about those pulling the strings in this circus. They did not appear to be soldiers, sailors or airmen, though all wore the insignia of commissioned officers. If one chanced to overhear snippets of conversation while socializing, the word 'thug' often cropped up. It was an offensive word used to distinguish between the commissioned and non-commissioned ranks in groups such as this one. It was an expression I had never heard of among combat formations, nor would it have been tolerated. The Rhodesian – the oldest – was indignant at being categorized as a thug and being controlled by a bunch of snotty 'bean pushers' (his words not mine). To placate him I said: 'If I were not here Jack, I would be somewhere else in this global war. It really isn't worth bothering about'. At heart, I felt

Jack was right. It was a stupid description and an inappropriate tag.

On the third night (19/20 January 1944) we made it through the hole in the floor about 1 a.m. The moon lit up the frosty ground below. Dangling from my 'chute I surveyed with horror the rooftops of a small town and a jumble of electric lights on the north edge. As the last to jump, I saw our three containers follow us out, to drift clear of the houses. Apart from a few bullets that whizzed by, my senses told me this was not our destination. The other two were coming down, it seemed, among the houses.

I lay still on landing at the edge of what seemed to be a playground. I needed time to gather my senses but a sudden roar of engines brought me to my feet. Three Halifax bombers appeared low over the area and began unloading what I took to be supplies for the partisans. They were not part of our outfit, although maybe they were the part we didn't 'need to know' about. The containers were the same as ours, all weighing in the region of 350 lbs, fixed to parachutes. They rained down over a wide area, some landing on rooftops, some drifting to smash into windows. The 'bean pushers' were certainly having a ball tonight, a ball the residents would never forget. I could hear screaming and shouting: the whole town had been wakened.

Inwardly cursing, I wrapped up my 'chute, tucked it under a bush, and made for the open ground in the direction of our own containers. The one containing my radio was clearly marked, but someone else was heading in the same direction. This was no time to start shooting – he could be a partisan. He turned out to be a Yugoslav, but no partisan. More like a civil policeman. He tried frantically to tell me something. '*Nimski ovde*,' he kept repeating, pointing in the direction of the road. My smattering of Serbo-Croat did not extend to that vital word for Germans. 'Germans here' was what he was trying to tell me. With hindsight perhaps he knew this was a trap and was doing his best to warn me. A group of soldiers were getting nearer, and he darted off towards the town and I to some trees near the road, to try and identify the soldiers.

69

They were not wearing the German tin hats, but soft hats similar to those worn by the Yugoslavs I had trained with.

Taking a chance, I broke cover and joined them, filling the empty space in the last line of three and continued to double along with them for some distance. The soldier on my right looked inquiringly at me, expecting a response. I said: '*Ya sam Englasko*'. Startled, he shouted an order and within seconds there were so many gun muzzles stuck in my waist. A thought crossed my mind: one false move on my part and this trigger-happy bunch might open fire and my torso fall off. I recall the moment well; it conjured up cartoon-like humour, but not for long, as I was forcibly propelled to their HQ. Literally by gun muzzles.

The first thing I noticed in the lighted room were the canvas belts we had been issued with: the other two had already passed this way. By each belt, its contents were neatly stacked: a pile of gold coins (20 franc Napoleons) and wads of paper money. My captors were German and by all accounts had hit the jackpot.

Inscribed on the buckles of their belts were the words '*Gott Mit Uns*'. The officer who appeared to be in charge said, 'How many more?'

'Only three,' I replied.

'You lie!' he shouted. My hands were still above my head; to them I was not just a stray bean dumped among them, I was something far more sinister. To fool around was to commit suicide and promotion for the first man to pull a trigger. The officer came forward to remove my belt. Attached to it was a pouch that held batteries and a wire that led to a signalling lamp tucked away in my trouser pocket. Someone shouted, bomb, or something like it. There was a rush to the door, though the officer remained, the blood drained from his face. He held his gun firmly to my chest and muttered something like 'don't be a fool', and called to the last retreating figure to come back. With trembling hands he removed the pouch, my belt, and a .32 pistol and ammo strapped to a holster under my arm, before returning his gun to its holster. We both felt better; when our eyes met again

70

there was a kind of appreciation for each other.

From my belt came more Napoleons, a volt meter, radio crystals and a handful of condoms. Gently, a soldier raised a sachet to the light and whispered in almost disbelief, 'Englisher Brief'. In the silence that followed a compulsion to correct him came over me, and I blurted out: 'No! No! French brief'. At that, they burst out laughing. At least it established we had something in common.

My next stop was what I took to be the station commander's office. The commandant reminded me of a Major we used to call Daddy, in the early days of war and the Militia. He asked the escort to leave the room, and as the door closed pointed to a chair and offered me a cigarette.

'Young man, why have you come here?' he asked.

'I don't know where I am except that you have set a trap and we have dropped in it,' I replied.

'This is Kŏcevje. Where were you supposed to drop?'

'It is impossible to fix anything on this job.'

'But there must have been a reason for coming to this part of Yugoslavia?'

'Yes', I replied, 'to help the Yugoslav army of liberation.'

Half closing his eyes he became exasperated. In a louder tone of voice said, 'And now you are in a very dangerous position and could be shot. There is no army of liberation, only bandits, and that is what you will be tried as. All of you will be classed the same as any other bandit.' He pressed a buzzer, the escort returned, and led me out to join the other two. Jack and the Captain were surprised to see me, they had thought I had got away.

We were treated well, given the same food as the army. There was a bathroom, toilet, three beds and a large window overlooking the countryside, all prepared as if they were expecting guests. From this window we could see a small pickup truck daily bringing in containers. Many had broken open spilling uniforms, boots, small arms and mines among other things. These were not part of our operation, but who among them would believe that in the final analysis?

There were no restrictions on conversation and when we did

settle down to talk about our future there were no attempts to apportion blame. We all knew at heart, somewhere down the line, we had walked into this with our eyes open, albeit blind to the consequences of being caught red-handed doing what good soldiers ought not to be doing. No deals were mentioned.

Privately, I recalled the words of a headhunting Major who interviewed me six weeks after the Battle of El Alamein. I wondered about the Captain and Jack.

On the fifth day and taking no chances, our captors paraded about 20 armed escorts, maybe fearing a partisan rescue attempt, and marched us about a mile to a small airstrip where a tiny aircraft stood. The pilot demanded that we be tied up. They had no handcuffs, so our wrists were tied together with string. Then we were stacked, one behind the other, like sardines, leaving barely enough room for the pilot. He squeezed in, muttering, but did not share the good humour and banter that many of our captors were exchanging at his predicament. It was an amusing scene that tempted me to raise my arms while laughing as the plane took off.

Looking down on the rugged hills that are part of the Balkan mountain range it was easy to see the difficulties the German army faced in trying to control the region and how easy it was for the partisans to disrupt the German efforts.

Landing at Zagreb airport I looked around, for I had decoded a message only a few days prior to the bean pushers' ball, giving a rundown on this airport. It was nice to know some beans were here, watching. From a truck parked on the edge of the field a posse of six soldiers came toward us, removed the string round our wrists and fastened handcuffs, then linked the handcuffs with a chain. With our hands in front of us we walked towards the covered truck and were unceremoniously bundled into the back, followed by four guards to keep watched over us, and then departed.

Just before it got dark the lorry stopped outside the front entrance to an hotel. Opening the back a soldier said, 'Welcome to Ljubljana'. Here we were interrogated by Gestapo officers, in what I took to be a lakeside hotel. Other forms of the German security services also got in on the act. In many ways I could see the similarities that existed between our two services. Even to throwbacks to the Kaisers who strutted in wearing khaki riding breeches with a broad red stripe and a chest bedecked with orders, rows of medals and grey handlebar moustache. They got short shrift from the interrogating officers present.

Hours later, and separately, we were taken to the local jail and put in separate cells. We had been stripped of all our possessions down to a handkerchief, and the cells were bare but for a straw mattress. This must surely be the end of the ball.

If operation 'Volt' (the word defined as the unit of electromotive force) initially meant anything, it was by now a dead cell, about to be discarded. We had been summarily charged as spies and bandits to be held in a civil prison without POW status until a judicial trial could be arranged.

Next morning we left Ljubljana handcuffed, chained and clutching a flat round loaf of bread. We were bundled once more into the back of an open pickup and set off, this time with Gestapo guards who forbade any form of communication. Taking my bearings from sun and shadow I soon realized we were heading in a northerly direction. The countryside was beautiful. Frozen snow patches and icicles hung from trees, and took my mind back to my stay in Cairo when I was informed of one of the dominant features of winter in Yugoslavia, the 'Bura'; a north wind, originating in the area of the Barents Sea, that froze everything in its path, similar to the frozen March winds from the east that swept across southern England and made life on our farm pretty miserable. Now we sought shelter behind the truck's headboard and were thankful when the truck turned off towards a cluster of buildings. There were more guards at the gates and the cluster of low gray buildings, hoary with age, presented a forbidding picture.

We were unchained but left cuffed, and yanked off the truck and quickly led to the entrance and along passage after passage until we reached a guarded gate. An exchange of

73

documentation went on while others stood by with guns at the ready pointing at us as we passed through what I could only imagine as the gates of hell, into another passage with doors along its length. At door number four I was literally pushed across the floor and the door slammed behind me.

Still handcuffed but clutching my loaf of bread (my fingers had more or less stuck in it for warmth) I surveyed my new home. For heating there was a cast-iron domed object, whatever was used to keep it going was inserted from the passage. The room was roughly ten feet long by eight wide with a barred window, then iron bars and an inner window, which opened inward, and was fixed in a wall two feet thick. A wooden stool was the only piece of furniture. There was a pile of sacking in one corner, and by the cell door was a smaller door, behind which was a compartment that housed a bucket for the needs of nature. There was a single, lit bulb, whose fitting was screwed to the ceiling.

The clatter of boots heralded the return of the jailers, and the door was flung open. The inevitable array of gun muzzles appeared, and a guard removed my cuffs. Without a word the door slammed once more to leave me to ponder on an uncertain future. About every half hour a click at the door meant the spyhole had been opened, then in the silence that followed tapping on the walls from adjacent cells would commence. It took a day or two to realize this was a form of communication like 'good morning' or 'goodnight' or 'hahaha' and so on. I learned to recognize the ups and downs of life in adjacent cells, and even the gender of the occupants; women tended to tap lighter, and when they were let out to the toilet, they invariably had something to say to the guard.

There were other routines. Each morning the door would open and the guard would call 'Abort'. That meant a visit to the toilet situated at the end of the passage. On a ledge were placed piles of pages, torn from children's books, to be used as toilet paper. I would bring a few sheets back to my cell to read. They contained universal children's stories written in German that helped me practise the language. The toilet was a throne-like edifice facing the door with a spy hole, but it was a place visited by every prisoner in that row. Time, to these guards, appeared too precious, and lingering was not tolerated.

These trips were also interesting, though they were never made without a gun pointing at you. The guards were not part of the Wehrmacht (regular army) but from the security services controlled by the Gestapo. They put a God-like fear into the hearts of the Yugoslav workers and prisoners who, when spoken to, replied, '*Ya Miester*'. So whatever I did, I did with caution.

The writing on doors of the cells gave some indication as to the plight of the occupier. On my door was written '*Banditen*' (pronounced Ban-dee-ton). Other writings I did not fully understand but clearly they were all punishment cells. The worst you could have written on your door was '*Drie Tag Nix Essen*'. At first sight I guessed it was the end. The occupant was for the chop and had three days with no food to think about it.

Then came the morning wash. If your stool was not in front of the door the bowl was dumped on the floor. The water was cold. There was no soap, no towel, no toothbrush or razor or any human convenience. I used my shirt to rub my skin dry then put it on the iron dome to dry. Breakfast followed with a 'shale' (pronounced–sharlay): a small metal bowl holding about a pint of luke-warm tea (no milk or sugar). Again, if the stool was not by the door the shale and a small portion of bread went on the floor. The morning routine was completed about 9 a.m. All that was left was to shake out the fleas from the three bits of sacking that served as blankets, and fold them up to make a comfortable seat and sit back against the wall. From this position I would dream and plan a possible means of getting in touch with the other two or a possible route of escape should a stray bomb hit the place.

I had established that my window faced approximately south-east. Triest, I figured, would be the best destination, almost 25 miles due south. Mulling over these possibilities used up time and I was thankful for the hours I spent in Cairo studying maps of the area.

The midday shale contained about a pint of swede soup. It never varied. The soup was almost as clear as water, and we got the same in the evening but with a piece of bread. To think back on the acres of swedes grown on the farms in Sussex and put into clamps for winter cattle feed – here I was drinking the water the swedes were boiled in!

Abort time came round again about 5 p.m. The doors opened from one to ten, but sometimes in reverse order. This meant the other two must pass my door on their way to the toilet. The guards varied, the Captain spoke German and must have put communication high among his priorities. A week had passed, and I had waited by the door on each occasion. Then it happened. The Captain called, 'Above the light'. The guard shouted for silence and gave me a dirty look when it came to my turn. The toilet door locked behind me, I looked up to the light and there a piece of paper was lodged. With my belt I knocked the paper down, put it in my pocket, sat on the throne and looked for a more convenient postbox, like a crack in the wall. back in my cell, concealed from the door, I read the note. 'We must communicate. Suggestions?' The following day he got my message as he passed my door. 'Crack in wall'. My door received a thump for silence but the abort post came into being and was used almost every day thereafter and from it learned Jack occupied Cell 7 and the Captain Cell 10.

As days became weeks, a regular course in German came through the post from cell number ten: the Captain's. This additional help got me translating bits of conversation that went on between the guards. While hunger and the growing number of fleas that sucked my blood through the long nights presented problems like 'how long can the human body continue to be a source of supply for thousands of these creatures?' and 'How long would it take me to search out and destroy them?' A very long time. This was time-consuming, but then, time was all I had, and it was something to do which was just what I needed.

With a small pencil I had concealed in my battle dress before setting out from Bari, I would write my daily letter in the margin of a page used for toilet paper, carefully tearing the margin from the page, and rolling it up ready for posting. At the end of each day, I marked down the flea kills on the wall chart and then carefully concealed both pencil and letter in different places in my clothes. But oh those nights of torture! The fleas were now crawling all over me, especially the centre of my back. These I could only crush by rubbing my back against the floorboards or against the wall. My shirt had stuck to my back with congealed blood. All those killed during the hours of darkness went unrecorded. Daytime kills included those scraped out of my developing beard and uncombed hair that fell into the washbasin, and these averaged around 80.

After about three weeks of silence, two guards entered my cell, and told me to get dressed. A few minutes later a Gestapo officer entered. 'You are required for interview,' he said, and pointed to the floor. With a guard on each side and the officer behind we went through passages and rooms. As it was around midday there was plenty of activity. We passed what I took to be inmates; the look in their eyes as we approached and the way they looked down as we passed made me realize this was a fearful place to be in, and not just for me.

The interview room was no bigger than my cell, with a table and four chairs and two other officers. The senior Gestapo officer (a Captain) pointed to a chair and sat on my right, with the Lieutenant on my left and what I took to be a warrant officer opposite with a typewriter. It was all very civil. The Lieutenant spoke. 'We are not interested in what you came to do, or intended to do. We already have sufficient evidence of your purpose. What we want to know is who you are'.

I was born in India, went to school in the Himalayas, and came to England to join my father on his farm, where I thought I had landed in the middle ages. There was no electricity, no mains water supply or sanitation. It was hard to believe that England was the hub of an Empire. Taking advantage of a pending war situation I joined the army, at

77

the time offering a trade in the Royal Signals as a wireless operator. My retired father was an ex-Captain, who had been awarded the OBE on retirement, which the family referred to as the 'Order of the Boot'. He lived at that time in East Sussex. I had two brothers; one a Captain in the West African Frontier Force and the other a Corporal serving in Burma. My younger two sisters were serving somewhere in India as Queen Alexander's Nursing sisters, and the eldest sister was an inspector in a munitions factory. What each were doing now I had no idea. Nothing was skipped. Slowly we progressed through our family history, my life at school and my journey to England in 1928 at the age of thirteen. It was important to establish that I was a serving soldier and nothing else. That was my defence. It did not matter if what I said was true or not, they were getting the picture.

Every so often a knock on the door gave some respite, and a soldier would enter, come to attention and bawl out '*Heil* Hitler!' and raise his arm in salute. All present (except me) rose and replied: '*Heil* Hitler'. The soldier would deliver his message, 'HH' again and depart. I had gone through two sessions of interrogation while in training, and knew that episodes like this were intended to frighten. Play dumb, don't stand up, they may wear you down in time, but answer freely any questions about your life. It puts them at ease. These questions took up 90 per cent of the information they required and as darkness approached I was thankful to be away from my cell and the fleas.

The soldier had been in twice, and here he was again with the same rigmarole but this time indicating a meal was ready. The Gestapo got up and left. I remained and my shale of swede soup and bread was put in front of me. The inmate who brought it swiftly departed as three gun-toting guards entered. I thought it might be a good idea to enter into conversation by mentioning the fleas in my cell, telling them my shirt was stuck to my back with congealed blood. They just laughed and went into an animated conversation, looking at me as if to say: 'Don't worry, it will be bullets that will put an end to the likes of you'. I conceded this to be typical behaviour of soldiers stationed in a hostile country that had suffered at the hands of the partisans, terrorists and saboteurs, and made no further effort to commune with them.

The Gestapo returned, and the guards moved out, my shale with them, taken by a petrified prisoner. In a casual manner the Lieutenant said: 'Good, now where were we?' adding 'Ah yes.' He appeared to be enjoying the opportunity to practise his English. 'What we cannot understand is how you three came to be together? You appear to have nothing in common!' This had crossed my mind from the very outset. He continued: 'All of you have been born or reared in different countries, you have served in different formations, and prior to the war, in different occupations. Yet you say you have never met them until six weeks before you left Bari. It just doesn't make sense'. But this was true.

I gave him a blank look, and then said: 'I wish I knew'.

The questions began to deal with my life in the Middle East during 1942 and 1943. The desert battles, Aleppo, our purpose there, its bars, brothels, cinemas, cafés, anywhere soldiers tended to frequent. Then I told them about Beirut, where soldiers spent their leave. My posting to Haifa and the parachute training battalion was covered, also Tel Aviv and Cairo. This was all part of my defence to prove that I had been employed as a soldier within specific military units – that I have never been seconded to a Special Service organization, trained or served with one. I conceded being transferred to the ISLD only six weeks before coming to Yugoslavia, but said that as I understood it I was to do the same work I had done both before and during the war to date: communications.

The questioning moved to my life as a soldier in India and my assignment as private radioman to a government political agent in Orissa in eastern India. Then I told them about my posting back to England as a technical instructor to the militia at the start of the war, and my training the militia in general army signal operations and becoming a Superintendent at NORCO.

At around midnight the 'HH' man came in to announce a

meal was ready, but not, of course, for me. I got the
inevitable shale with tea and was watched over by a different
set of guards, who did nothing to upset me. I felt satisfied
with my performance so far. The Gestapo Captain, it slowly
dawned on me, was from a legal department, sent here to
interview us and present our case to whatever court we were
destined for. I was sticking rigidly to my career in standard
military service (though being caught behind enemy lines with
a suitcase radio was not going to aid my case one bit). I tried
as hard as I could to keep my eye on the ball as the Gestapo
entered the room once more and the guards departed, my
shale with them.

'We are not satisfied with your answers,' said the
Lieutenant. 'You say you went on a parachute course. What
for? The war in the Middle East was over. You must have
been trained for this job?'

'No. The 11th Parachute Battalion was being formed in
Tripoli in north Africa, and there had been a parachute
training unit near Haifa for some time. All eyes were on
Europe and the second front.'

'Ah yes. The second front. When is that going to happen?'

They were now fishing, but once again a soldier interrupted
us and started the 'HH' routine. The senior officer just raised
his hand and brought it down in a gesture of dismissal. The
words of my tutor came back to me as he did this: just lead
the play; veer off the subject; time is on your side.

They had had enough. As he left the Lieutenant said: 'We
may meet again'.

As I entered my cell, dawn was breaking. I, too, had had
enough. I just flopped down on the sacking among the fleas
and went to sleep.

*

The daily routine did not change. At morning abort time I
was asleep and the guard came in, presumably to see whether
I was alive. I vaguely felt being prodded with a boot, and at
the same time someone shouted '*Raus*'. Opening my eyes all I

80

could see was the muzzle of a gun a few inches from my face. I instinctively pushed it roughly to one side. He jumped back shouting, and another guard came running in. I just lay there, tired, bewildered and lost for words with two guns pointing at me. I involuntarily raised my hands and uttered impatiently, '*Vas Ist*?' (what's the matter?). I really didn't care. The second guard said something and the two backed out.

It was around midday when the door opened again and a shale was dumped on the floor. I called, 'Abort *bitter*?' (toilet please). '*Spater*', (later) came the reply as the door shut. Spater, I discovered, meant never off schedule-times, but more often, never.

All that afternoon I spent picking fleas from my uniform. Within me there existed a mixture, elation, misery, hunger and a desire to reduce the population of fleadom. I felt elation at the way I had evaded being tripped up during my interrogation. A captured spy at the best of times usually ends up tied to a stake or something much worse. I accepted that, but felt there were grounds to be explored in my favour. I was no spy! I might be regarded as the biggest twit alive but should I end up at the stake for being one? All that mattered now was did my interrogators accept what I had to say? They were to be judge, jury, prosecutor and executioner. The holy badge on their belts was inscribed: '*Gott Mit Uns*' to remind them the Almighty was on their side.

On the down side I was living in this flea pit, without a change of clothes, a bath or decent wash, with little devils sucking my blood that were even at this moment concealed in my hair, clothes, blankets and with a million more beneath the floorboards awaiting their evening meal when sleep overcame my weakening frame. God, certainly, was not on my side.

I thought about this ever since I entered this cell. Though, inwardly I asked, 'Do I deserve this slow death?'. Aloud I replied, 'You dumb bastard, you volunteered for it'.

What was intended to be a private chat between me and my conscience attracted my neighbour from cell five who gave three taps (how are you). My three taps in return, starting low and moving up, meant I'm OK.

Later, putting my ear to the wall, the occupant of cell five appeared to be saying his prayers and crying. This was not unusual sometimes this agonizing pleading to an invisible icon came from cell three. Whatever faith I had in the Christian God was beginning to abate. I tapped three times, then again and in response the wall was slapped with both hands that slid down. The cries were louder. Whoever this person was, trouble was moving his way. Silence was all that I could offer, so that he could commune with his thoughts, or his maker.

Abort time was coming up. I wrote my note, re: my interrogation, and could the Captain check on door number five. The shale and bread came in, and I couldn't help comparing myself with the animals on our farm as I sat in the corner sipping from a tin bowl of swede soup and munching a piece of bread torn from its parent loaf. I concluded that the animals were better off.

Returning from the toilet I took a glancing look at door number five. On it was written: '*Drie Tag Nix Essen*' (three days no food). It could not mean anything else but the stake. 'Poor sod,' was all I could say. With the likes of us the authorities could do what they pleased – kill in any way they thought fit and dispose of the remains as was most convenient to them.

All next day I listened to his prayers, his sobs, his pleading at his cell door. All were to no avail. His shouts, that I took to be his last curses and insults to all men in heaven or on earth, attracted guards. Two went in, there was a 'thud', then silence.

What was happening served to emphasize the brutality the Nazi regime meted out to its subjects in occupied countries, and probably to their subjects at home. It was only now that I understood what this war was really all about. Hitler and his ilk had to be stopped. They were the evil gods that would have to be destroyed before sanity regained its place in human life.

On the following day the silence in number five was awful. I heard not a sound through the wall, and wondered if he had

82

resigned himself to his fate. It was hard to tell, until they came to take him away. There was no struggle, no last minute cry for mercy as the clatter of army boots faded along the corridor. I opened my inner window. The sun shone on this March or April day; time didn't matter. I didn't know or care what day it was or why the sun shone down on this evil world. A clear vision of what was taking place came before my eyes when the beat of a muffled drum set the pace for the firing squad on its short journey to the stake. Then silence. I waited for the burst of gunfire to reverberate around the prison. It came. Only one thing remained for me to consider: how would I take it when my turn came?

The Captain and I discussed this through the abort post. He told me of a conversation between two guards just outside his window after one such shooting. One said:

'Where do you aim?'

'At the chest!' he replied, 'and you?'

'At the head!'

More weeks went by. I was becoming desperate. I had lost count of time beyond a day, the flesh on my bones seemed to be withering away, and I discussed our chances of survival through the abort post with the Captain. We even debated whether we should refuse a blindfold when taken to the stake.

Somehow he managed to befriend one of the guards, for I received every few days a piece of bread, no bigger than what could nestle in the palm of a hand. I was so hungry I ravenously attacked that first morsel only to discover a handwritten note half chewed and indecipherable after I had spat it out. Unexpected, but marvellous, and I laughed at the cunning. It was the first laugh for at least ten weeks by my reckoning, and it did me more good than the extra bread. I did not thank him – not then, not through the abort post, but maybe we would all meet again.

Many things come in twos and threes. A week or so later I heard the sound of many feet come striding along the passage, stopping at my door. Opening it, a guard stepped in and shouted '*raus!*' Then, turning to the door, gave the 'HH' salute and in walked a very senior Gestapo officer. He was clearly shocked and called an interpreter who addressed the officer as *Herr Oberst* (Colonel). Then he asked. 'How are you?' What a bloody question I thought, but did my best to convey the life I was living in the cell, and Herr Oberst really looked around. Through the interpreter he asked many questions regarding my health, and he could see no attempts had been made to provide even the basic requirements. He called in another person who I took to be the equivalent of our regimental sergeant major, the ram-rod of this outfit, who referred to the officer as Herr Oberst General.

There must have been about six others in the Obersts' entourage. He spoke earnestly to the RSM and turning towards me offered a cigarette. Then he went to see the Rhodesian in number seven and the Captain in number ten.

Whatever else he was, he was a prime mover. That afternoon my cell floor was scrubbed with disinfectant, and a bed arrived with three blankets and a pillow. The next day I was stripped of all my clothes and given a sort of nightshirt, draped with a blanket and taken off to the shower baths while the gun-toting guards looked on, puzzled and a little subdued. That Oberst must have chewed somebody's balls off, for back in the cell a barber waited to cut my hair, shave me, and trim my toe and fingernails. That was not all – my uniform came back washed and ironed and when dressed I felt like a human being again.

Although the food did not improve, my health did. The fleas had been taking their toll, but with the cell floor washed and disinfected every three days they no longer presented a problem. The biggest surprise of all was being taken to a photographic room and photographed for the prison files. Now at least my name and likeness had been registered and I had become a person. At the end of May, after another shower bath, shave and haircut I was handcuffed and arrived at the entrance where the other two were waiting. Forbidden to talk we just looked at each other wondering what each had been through.

A pickup arrived with another set of soldiers, and one by one our cuffs were removed to be replaced by those belonging to the new escort. Documents were handed over and signed for, and that done we climbed aboard the best we could, lined up against the headboard as one of the guards produced a chain to link our cuffs and lock us to the ironwork of the truck.

Without any contact with the outside world since our capture on 19 January it was difficult to say what day it was. I had established our position in the vicinity of Bled, a small town in northern Slovenia, not far from the Austrian border, and almost due south of Klagenfurt, which had been bombed, according to some guards after an air-raid some weeks ago.

Where were we off to now? The journey took us to a railway station, and a guard went off to arrange a booking. There were a lot of people around, but none paid us any notice. When the guard returned we were quickly hustled onto a train, still chained, and handed over to two Gestapo officers in a compartment reserved for us. Only now were we informed that we were being taken to Vienna's *Untersucknungs Gefängnis* to await the outcome of a trial. We remained in cuffs and chained for the whole journey of approximately 125 miles, arriving in Vienna in the early afternoon. There was one thing about these Germans – they never considered their prisoners as anything other than baggage. We were given no food or water, nor allowed to go to a toilet until the train stopped at Vienna. Then there was the same routine – hustled through the crowd onto a truck and taken to the door of the prison. Only then, in the company of many guards, did the Captain get them to understand our needs. The old escort removed the chains and cuffs, handed over documents and left us in the hands of what seemed a more civilized bunch.

5

1944: The Year of my Life – Drie Englander

Our new guards led us up several flights of stairs, each flight opening up onto a wide, glass-fronted veranda. There were no cuffs or chains to cut into our wrists. About six flights up we walked along a veranda with regularly-spaced cell doors, many of which were marked with the letter 'O'. Two armed guards stood by an open door. The leading escort handing us over said: '*Drie Englander*', and the door shut firmly behind us.

What a surprise – three bunk beds complete with mattresses, sheets, blankets, a table, three chairs, washbowl and toilet. After five months solitary confinement in what I had suspected to be death cells, we were now able to talk freely, and it was hard to find words to express ourselves. Separately, we had undergone the same treatment, and now it was time to reflect on what had gone wrong as we awaited the verdict. Spy? Bandit? Terrorist? Or prisoner of war?

We were woefully ignorant of the happenings that had taken place since falling into German hands in January, even as to the date, the name of the day, or the month, only figuring that it must be around June to judge from the trees and shrubs in full leaf.

The preliminary attempts at conversation were broken by the sound of marching boots from the courtyard below. The guards down there were calling out '*Weg von Fenster*' (keep away from windows). To emphasize this, let off a few shots. But curiosity got the better of me, and climbing on to the top bunk slid forward until I could see a small part of the courtyard. To my surprise there were 20 or more German officers in full regalia walking in groups around an exercise yard. By the colour of the piping in their uniforms, they came

86

from many different branches of the army. The Captain and Jack wanted to see for themselves, each in turn giving their own commentary during the next 20 minutes. So many guards ready to shoot anyone foolish enough to look was a sure sign something important was cooking, apart from food. This was the *Untersuchnungs Gefängnis*, a holding prison for persons awaiting trial. Were these our judges? This gave us something to chew on.

The situation in January 1944: the German army was resisting Allied advances in Italy; the Russians had been advancing westward on a thousand-mile front; and no serious attempt to land on the western shores of Europe had been made by the Allies. That Germany was destined to lose this war was a conclusion most involved in the struggle had reached in 1943. But were the higher political figures in Germany cooking up reprisals with weapons of mass-destruction to further their aims, or were they simply collecting people like us to be used as hostages in the hope of making a deal?

They were known to be working on new weapons, and this accounted for the continuous stream of Special Forces doing what they could to locate, destroy, delay or prevent their completion. We were well aware of the existence of these 'executive operations', as they were called, that stretched from Greece to Norway, and many like us would have been caught, their fate unknown.

Again our animated discussion stopped abruptly as the flap in the door opened and a voice called: '*Essen*' (food). Our first meal of the day came on three trays. A mug of soup, a pack of Swiss cheese and a loaf of bread the size of a large bap. Over this we chatted in a more convivial way – civilization without eating irons added to the enjoyment of the meal. We even laughed at attempts at corny jokes until the flap opened once more, this time with the word '*Com*', and the trays were passed out. The Captain asked if he could have a newspaper and within a few minutes one was pushed through the door, dated 2 June 1944. We concluded we were in the hands of the regular German army, soldiers

87

with no party axe to grind.

Eagerly we devoured the news as the Captain interpreted item by item. Rome had fallen, the Russians had more or less overrun Yugoslavia, and we knew the Russians would make no deals over Allied hostages. They had suffered too much for that. Revenge, destruction and total surrender was what they wanted.

Days went by. The German officers did not return, and it was clear we were not going to enjoy a stroll on our veranda, though the daily paper kept coming to keep us abreast of what the German public were reading. That was the extent of our room service; we never saw the face of one guard, or heard the voice of another person. With so few words spoken it was difficult to know when duty shifts changed. There was no telling when or if bombs would drop on this place and give us a chance of escape.

During breakfast on the morning of 6 June around 8.30 a.m. a piece of creased paper was pushed under the door. I pounced on it, brought it to the table to read, 'The invasion has started'. It was written in English.

'Well, Well, there were beans here too. In the heart of the German Reich, keeping tabs on us.'

Our problem was exercise. The cell was so small that two had to lie on the bunks while the third walked the five or six paces to and fro, stopping to do a few physical jerks as a diversion. However, it didn't take long to get up a sweat as the sun warmed up the prison walls. With the only window wide open but facing the enclosed exercise yard and no through draft, the heat rising from the courtyard made the afternoons almost unbearable. Each day's routine after two weeks was getting synonymous with that of a caged animal. I had an aversion from childhood at seeing animals caged, and now here I was experiencing those same feelings those animals must have experienced walking the length of their cages.

In India, there had been dancing bears, performing monkeys tethered by chains, and snake charmers with cobras in baskets. I saw all these in the Simla hills, where I went to school. In England I hated the circus and the zoo, and now we were behaving in the same way as caged animals. Walking to and fro, sitting docile or lying down seeking forgetfulness in sleep.

The next event came in the form of an elderly person entering our cell; he introduced himself as a representative of the Swiss Red Cross. He waited for the door to shut behind him, then said:

'Please do not ask me any questions,' and handed us forms to fill in and sign. Number, rank, name, and signature. When all were safely back in his hands he pronounced us registered 'prisoners of war'. Then he produced letter paper and envelopes saying, 'I'll be back tomorrow'. He tapped on the cell door and departed.

This information gave us no reason to rejoice, but it did trigger off a discussion about that all-important interrogation at the prison near Bled. It was amazing to discover how little we knew about our mission, its purpose, or each other. Each had concealed private codes. Mine was still sewn in one of my battledress epaulettes. Only the bean pushers knew our intended purpose. But it took the German military judicial system to bring us back from the stake we once thought was our destination. We had been through severe hardship and came out without a harsh word spoken between us. Perhaps this was the reason why we were put together, three beans in a pod. When released, I suppose, the bean pushers hoped we would strike roots of our own, develop individually and contribute separately to military intelligence.

For the next week we remained as caged animals dwelling on thoughts of what was to become of us with the consolation that whatever we did, others would know that we had been here. Right now that seemed unimportant, as life in this cell was becoming as unhealthy as the last one, not physically but mentally. Only the newspaper gave us hope, and its content slowed down the rate of our declining sanity.

On the last day of June the door bolts were drawn back and the door swung open. A jailer, hidden from view, called: '*Aus tretten*' (step out). The sun, the air, the view were all beautiful: to feel the warm rays of the sun, to breathe the air and take in the beauty of what still remained part of an insane world, touched all my senses. It was a moment of freedom. However, being guided down by four gun-toting guards to ground level was all the freedom we were going to get. The sight of another set of guards waiting with handcuffs was no surprise. It appeared there was to be no let-up on us, though our Captain started a legal discussion on the treatment of POWs and the Geneva Convention with the prison officer. That officer, unconcerned, quoted an order that stemmed from a raid on Dieppe where captured Germans were left in chains after the raiders had gone. Because of that, he said, we too sometimes find it necessary to restrict the movement of certain prisoners. The discussion was academic; the cuffs stayed on.

A lorry stood at the entrance. In it were three Americans also handcuffed and looking very unhappy. We took our places opposite them: a Colonel and two Captains, they had been captured in Hungary, I guessed on a mission similar to ours. We exchanged names just in case any mishap might separate us: opposite me was Captain Suarez, the name I still remember, who turned out to be the groups' radioman.

There wasn't much talk at first. What held us back was hard to tell, perhaps being suspicious of each other or perhaps just different nationals cautious of each others' views or maybe we were just reluctant because we had not spoken to or seen anyone from our side for six months. The presence of two guards did not encourage conversation either. The journey was a short one. We stopped at the gates of an open prison. Long wooden huts, wire cages, and lookout towers were dotted around the perimeter fence. Just inside the gates was the main guardroom and a substantial cell block. The path to the door was lined with armed soldiers; no doubt the commandant had been forewarned of the arrival of a bunch of desperados. At the door our cuffs were removed. I was surprised at this show of force as we entered the cell block, but then, they were not to know that we were like the Biblical tares, or mixed seeds, of this war, carefully screened, nurtured, and then scattered in the hope of landing on fertile soil in which to put down our roots. We were the ones that fell on stony ground. Never to grow, never to flourish or to bear fruit. Never to wear medals.

The Americans were put in one cell while we three were incarcerated at the other end of the corridor, also in one cell. The cell had a raised platform that sloped upwards to the outside wall where a headboard similar to a scaffold plank served as a pillow and a bed for three with three sets of two blankets. Between the foot of the bed and the cell door was a space of one yard with a table and a chair.

We went for three days without meeting a soul other than guards who escorted us to and from the toilets and washroom, where soap, towels and safety razors were available courtesy of the Red Cross.

Our cell had one barred window looking out onto a road, and beyond was a wide expanse of farmland with ripening corn, a beautiful sight that brought back memories of the corn fields at home, only these were colossal by comparison. At home, I used to stroll through the fields with a girlfriend of an evening, grasp a handful of wheat ears, rub them in the palms of the hand and sample the tasty grain. In contrast, just over the road was a swimming pool in which the occasional *fraulein* would disport herself among young soldiers, and this was infinitely more interesting. Whatever the age of the female she was aware of the penetrating eyes of the sex-starved prisoners that followed her every move and I believe, she enjoyed every moment of it.

The big surprise came in the form of Red cross food parcels – gifts from the people of America, Britain and Canada. I came to realize these gifts saved thousands of POWs from death and possible post-war ills due to malnutrition. They contained food we had only dared to dream of: meat, powdered milk, chocolate, boiled sweets, all of which we should have rationed to allow our digestive systems to cope. But it was like Christmas, and we were behaving like kids searching through a box of presents. I sat back against the wall to nibble a bar of chocolate. Jack and the Captain did very much the same, with the goodies of their choice, until the mechanism of our digestive systems began to break down. The Americans were going through a similar but less violent bowel upheaval – perhaps they had not been deprived for as long as we, or had greater will-power, but they did not escape the torment that took place in the bowels. The German sergeant, probably gasping for fresh air, relented and let us out to an exercise cage where at last we were able to let off wind unashamedly to be dispersed by a light breeze that wafted away the stinking cannonades of hot air. Talk and laughter erupted into friendship brought about by the human urge to compete in this and to learn something about each other. Protocol had broken down.

Each day after that we came out for one hour but not at specific times, and greeting each other like buddies. The inevitable discussion of future opportunities available when the war ended took place. Although I had obtained top qualifications in the army they might not be considered for civilian employment. I had no desire to return to farming, and had a yearning to get into civil aviation. For this I would have to compete with airforce radiomen. I recall four of us sitting in the corner of the pen, our backs resting up against the wire languishing in the Austrian sun, musing on employment after the war, when Suarez said in a casual manner: 'Rob, when you go for that job, talk only to the man at the top. He is the only one who can say yes or no'. That bit of advice stayed with me. I practised it and passed it on to younger people who sought my advice.

As the days went by, note paper and pencils became available. As both our Captain and Captain Gray, an American, spoke German fluently, I was keen to learn. Captain Gray advised not to learn from the guards, because they were from rural areas with numerous dialects. He could hardly recognize the language they spoke as German. Well, he obviously had never travelled around England where dialects were equally various and, at times, unrecognizable as English!

There were several guards, some were not unfriendly. The one I chose to work on was married, two children, pushing forty with little interest in the war. As a family man he

92

welcomed conversation as well as I did, to improve my German. When I broached the subject of 'Booze for chocolate' he showed interest and was prepared to do anything to brighten his drab lifestyle. On his next turn at guard duty, he would be patrolling beneath the cell block windows. He wanted chocolate and I wanted booze. The only drink he could get hold of was schnapps. I had never heard of it, but it would have to do. So it was agreed one block of chocolate for one bottle of schnapps. I gave my word that no attempt would be made to jump him, and delivery was to take place at midnight. The chocolate was to be put on the table by the door where the exchange would take place and we must be lying on our beds. This entrepreneur must have been a general trader in the open camp, as he was taking no chances.

Lying awake I heard the key turn and saw the door slowly open and a hand reach out to take the chocolate and then put a bottle in its place. The door closed silently and the key turned once more. We sat up and passed the bottle round toasting ourselves, and didn't leave out Tito, who I suppose would have been our commander in different circumstances. The booze was nothing to write home about – I suspected he brewed the stuff himself.

Trading in this block, he said, was too risky for him. This was understandable, as a report had filtered through that someone had tried to assassinate Hitler. That was enough to make any German jumpy. But the story of the trade filled a page, and my tutors made their comments. Several more tit-bits of this sort almost filled an exercise book by the end of our stay.

It appeared the cells were being filled by others, though we never got to meet them, but we guessed they visited the cage as a boulder was left there on one occasion. As a result, a contest took place of putting the shot. After a practice watched by the American Colonel (who took no part until we had three attempts each) Captain Suarez nudged me and said, 'Watch this'. This Colonel picked up the boulder, and with no fancy preliminaries putt it almost a metre beyond the best.

There was something about that Colonel that commanded my respect and certainly the respect of Captain Suarez. The Colonel was tall and wiry, hardly smiled and said little. He called everyone by their surname. I never got to know his name.

We were now into August and harvest time. A sight once common in rural England prior to the 1920s was on view in the corn field opposite. Cutting large stands of corn with scythes, four stalwarts were moving forward in echelon, their scythes swinging in unison. At each pass of the scythe they gathered a bunch of straw stalks and laid them flat, forming four swaths in neat rows. After a while others moved in. It took best part of an hour to circumvent the field before pausing to sharpen their blades, chat, have a drink and rest. The men, in trousers and singlet-type vests and coloured sweat bands round their necks, were all masters of their craft, and were joined by women, wearing head scarves and colourful gypsy skirts who immediately started tying the straw into sheaves, standing them upright in stooks of six or eight sheaves to allow the eares (seed heads) to dry out. These scenes held my attention until dusk. A guard informed me they were Romanians or Hungarians also prisoners.

A new sergeant arrived straight from the Russian front, sporting the Iron Cross and badges for bayonet charges, grenade-throwing and hand-to-hand fights. He was a young man, proud to be in the German army, proud to be German and ready to die for his country, and presumably for the Führer as well. He was not to be messed with but did his duty without malice though he was suffering from war fatigue or shock. Wherever he stood outside he appeared to be gazing into a world he would like to be in. His head would shake, alternately nodding and then going from side to side. It was easy to see that he had been through hell. We knew this soldier, blinded by duty, oblivious to what was happening to his country and countrymen, remained a believer in the Führer. A French sergeant major who had arrived and was locked up in the adjacent cell to us dubbed him '*Oui et non*' (yes and no).

94

During September the three Americans and us *Drie Englanders* were told to take whatever food we had and get ready to move. We were then handcuffed and led outside to be joined by an English Brigadier and a private, both captured in Albania, and two English sergeants captured in Serbia while serving in one of General Mihailovich's Cheta's (known as chet'niks). All were handcuffed in pairs. The German camp commandant of Stalag XVII A arrived to hand us over to a Gestapo warrant officer who demanded our identity discs. There was a heated exchange between the camp commandant, a Colonel in the Wehrmacht and the Gestapo warrant officer; the warrant officer got his way. Ignoring the Colonel from the Wehrmacht and ordering his own men to remove our discs, saying: 'Should any trouble arise we will shoot you'.

This display of authority was watched by the camp guards who appeared visibly frightened of our new bodyguards, and without so much as a salute to the senior officer present the warrant officer gave the order to move out. This example of military discipline was just another omen of the loosening ties that bound this once invincible military machine.

Stopping in a railway yard we were bundled out and told to board a rail box wagon that held two bales of straw, and had a small window 25 inches high by 12 wide, high up in one corner. Even the tallest needed to stand on a straw bale to see out. It was in fact a cattle or cargo box wagon, but with a difference: graffiti in the form of names and dates adorned almost every inch of its sides.

Before the last guard departed our cuffs were removed, and a bucket of water and the inevitable shale were provided, before the sliding door slammed home and was bolted.

We travelled all night. Early next morning we were let out in twos to relieve ourselves by the side of the track, watched by a guard. No extra time was allowed to stretch one's legs – it was back into the box as each pair completed the necessary bodily function. The doors closed and the train moved slowly northwards.

The prison we had just left was Stalag XVII A, a prison camp for soldiers under officer rank. The Germans had made no attempt to separate our group – they treated us all the same. Casting my mind back to the night of my capture and the Major's words, 'This is Kočevia and you are bandits and will be treated as bandits, all of you, and you could be shot'. We were certainly not out of the woods yet.

The Brigadier hogged the window more than he should have, which caused a certain amount of tension. Shenton, one of the sergeants captured in Serbia, had a repertoire of ribald songs that included those sung by the Yugoslav partisans, and he managed to get most of us to join in. He even managed to persuade the Brigadier to come away from the window and let some air in. The Americans became keen participants too. Whatever barriers of rank that might have existed, sergeant Shenton had removed them.

At midday the train stopped, the door slid back and we were ordered out, the man adding '*mit Essen*' (with food). The Germans supplied nothing to eat, only water to drink. The guards spread out to a safe distance in a well practised manner, allowing us a limited amount of freedom, at the same time giving them a defence against surprise attack. It seemed this was a well-known stopping place as one of the guards asked if we had any money as there was a beer house nearby. Only Captain Suarez had managed to hold on to some Deutschmarks. How? He never let on, but he was persuaded to part with some. The rest of us didn't have a sou between us. I wondered how Suarez managed to get his pile, but it wasn't important; just our good luck he had some for a bottle of beer each.

For three hours or more we basked in the afternoon sun stripped to the waist, chatting, laughing and joking, when finally the order was given to return to the box. It seemed strange this one box and one passenger carriage with twice as many guards as prisoners was still going north. Were we prize captives destined for exhibition, to be traded for others, or what? My dream that night as I lay in the straw against the inside of the box jolting along was a particularly bad one. We had been taken to a place of execution, where, one by one the Germans hauled us up by the neck to be left to die. This had one spark of defiance as my eyes were clouding over, a voice from one of the near dead croaked: 'Sing us a song Shenton'.

Sitting up with a jerk, I looked around. Bodies lay sprawled, curled, half sitting, with head bent forward on raised knees, all like ghosts in the dawn light that filtered through the small window to defuse and silhouette the still figures spread across the floor. It took a few moments to recover, to realize, like the many other dreams that had haunted my nights in this war, it was all a hoax and only the beads of sweat that broke away to join others that trickled down my face and neck were real.

The noise trains make when crossing points and travelling at a slow pace caused some to stir, and someone looking through the window said, 'We're in a marshalling yard'. With bumps and jerks and shunting the train finally came to rest and the doors were pulled back. The order, '*Bleiden*' (stay put) came loud and clear. Other guards came in, handcuffed us in pairs once more, and led us to something that looked like market stalls covering an acre or more where we were invited to wash, bathe and launder our clothes under taps spaced about a metre apart. It reminded me of a place behind the lines at El Alamein in the western desert of Egypt; a man-made oasis for thousands of troops pulled out of the line for 24 hours to wash away the louse-ridden sand that crept into every crevice of the human body. That had been a place of sunshine, joy and laughter. Here, the crude provisions were anything but a joy. I couldn't help wondering who before us had passed this way? With all that graffiti in one box wagon, there must have been trainloads of prisoners and this must be a transit station. I looked into the face of the train driver. He seemed to be looking at us with interest. How many stories that driver could tell I'd never know. We were now in Dresden's railway marshalling yard. This was not encouraging; we were also nearer to the Russian armies. Although the Russians were our allies, I felt more vulnerable. Stories were beginning to be circulated through the daily papers of Russian behaviour. In my own mind, Russia and its people had little to thank Britain or its empire for. I wanted

97

to get as far away from them as I did from the Germans, who now held me prisoner.

For the first time the group were separated into two parties and without any preliminaries the six officers were led away and the five other ranks followed at some distance behind. At the edge of the yard two small trucks stood with about four guards by each. The officers were handcuffed and climbed into one while we climbed into the other, also handcuffed. The trucks parted company.

It wasn't long before I realized we were heading in an easterly direction, and the officers' truck was nowhere to be seen. The journey took about an hour and then we pulled into what looked like a bus depot. Then we set off on foot up a narrow road with one guard in front, one at the side and two behind. Eventually we arrived at the gateway of an ancient castle, complete with portcullis and an iron gate with spikes pointing upward, outward and downward.

No knights in shining armour could possibly enter this castle uninvited, but for us the iron gate creaked and squeaked as it was pulled open and the portcullis rose as two soldiers cranked the wheel. It would have gone down well if we were a bunch of tourists; it was certainly a curiosity.

'Welcome to *Königstein Shloss*,' said one of the gate guards as we were led in. The castle appeared empty though there were signs of human life; kiddies toys on a green lawn, a washing line with clothes hanging on it, all signs of normal family life. Other soldiers appeared, and they seemed surprised and gathered round, perhaps wondering what fish pond we had been hooked from.

A sergeant, a member of the castle defence force, called to the escort, '*Herein, Kasematte Fier*' (this way, casement number four) and led us down to a walled enclosure with only a dozen or so English soldiers housed in a sort of bunkhouse. They appeared quite content with their lot, having been captured in the Egyptian desert, filtered through Italy and Austria into Germany and ended up not far from the Polish border. Nothing much went on here, they said. Eat, play cards, play football in a very confined area.

The prisoners were all infantrymen, some from a Sussex regiment that disappeared during the battle of El Alamein in 1942. Bunk beds were supplied in a building that can only be described as a lean-to. But why were they here? Penned up with only the sky and the swastika flag that flew over the battlements for scenery.

What were the Germans contemplating? The question kept recurring. The two newspapers sent down at breakfast time kept us informed. Half the inmates had learned German. Meals were properly supervised and regular Red Cross parcels really added to the well-being of each individual. The camp commandant visited the casement every other day with someone called the *Sonderführer* (interpreter). No guards entered the casement during daylight hours; they occupied a piece of land overlooking the casement during the day. At night the bunkhouse Billies were locked in, and a guard patrolled the casement.

Then a sort of pantomime took place between the POWs locked in and the German guard locked out. Songs were sung like 'soon we'll be on the outside looking in and you'll be on the inside looking out'. There were cat-calls, and obscenities. In the still of the night when the guard was least expecting trouble, a loud animal screech would penetrate the night, the sound waves bouncing off the walls. My hair stood on end the first time I heard the screech. The guard let out a string of swear words and threatened to shoot the '*Schweinhund*' (pigdog). They were probably grade C troops and this was a cushy number for them, where no one ever got shot or even heard a shot fired in anger.

Only once did I get on top of the battlements and was surprised to find a flat surface resembling the flight-deck of an aircraft carrier. I supposed small aircraft could land and take off. There was a spectacular view of the west side of the River Elbe where a very large stone that probably once bridged the river could be seen.

We stayed for four or five weeks, and during that time I played bridge and chess, and competed in a few bouts of boxing. After a week, the late arrivals were summoned to the commandant's office. On his desk was my exercise book. He told me this was a Saxon castle and that I, an Anglo-Saxon, could have stemmed from these parts. He seemed particularly interested in the trading activities at Stalag XVII A. 'Surely German soldiers don't do this sort of thing, this cannot be true?' He was a proper daddy and shook his head when I replied that it happens in every army. My book was never returned to me.

In mid-October we were assembled and told to get ready to leave. The commandant, a Major by rank, seemed genuinely sorry to see his boys go and wished them a safe return home to England. Whether he included us five newcomers was hard to tell, but he was a kind soul who waved us goodbye as we passed through his fortress gateway. I believe this establishment was not listed as a Stalag or Oflag, though the German sergeant told me that high ranking civil and military personnel had been held prisoner in the castle.

The descent on foot gave me an opportunity to take in the scenery, and there was general chatter that exploded into bursts of laughter. No one had mentioned our destination, and if the almost wet eyes of the commandant were anything to go by as he waved farewell, he had some misgivings. With Russians rolling in from the east, the Allies from the west, the Wehrmacht (a proud, brave, confused and wounded army) were taking daily punishment from both, and we were a bunch of strays mixed up in the middle. This was no recipe for a safe return to England.

At the bottom of the hill we boarded a bus, seemingly on a scheduled run. A woman got on, and seemed surprised to see the bus full of POWs. With all eyes on her, she paused. A guard nodded to her to board. The woman was near me, so I offered her my seat. Someone called, 'You crafty sod'. The bus stopped at Dresden station. No one moved except the woman, with all heads leaning into the gangway to watch her every movement. At the door she turned and gave us the faintest of faint smiles of the Mona Lisa variety before disappearing from our lives.

Waiting for us were more guards to take us to our next

destination wherever that was going to be. Rather than linger in the open, we were ushered into the waiting room on the station platform. It was large, with a restaurant bar, and was more than half full of civilians. The staff, apparently used to this type of intrusion, quickly shuffled people around to make a safe area in view of the guards stationed at each exit. One of the bunkhouse Billies asked for tea. 'Only ersatz,' said the waitress. Diving into his rucksack he said, 'I have tea, sugar and milk'. His long stay as the guest of the German Reich had not been wasted. He spoke the language well, albeit with a Lancashire accent which brought smiles to many faces. A buzz went up among the civilians, mostly elderly people, as the soldier handed over the goods from his Red Cross parcel. The staff wasted no time in laying the table with cups and saucers. Before leaving I noticed several bunkhouse Billies were discreetly handing over items of food. The gesture, like daddy's on the hill, was just plain human kindness.

The people sitting in the cafe wore expressions as if they had problems just living. To see prisoners with tea and sugar merely piled on the agony. This area had so far escaped the pounding of the British and American Airforces, and these civilians harboured no illusions that it would stay that way. The war was getting nearer each day.

An army canvas-covered lorry took us on our next leg going west. Any relevant question was met with the standard answer: '*Spater*' (later). After two hours, the lorry stopped outside the gates of a very large country manor house, on a hill overlooking the town. 'Colditz castle' someone said. It looked nothing like the real Macoy that we had just left.

With little delay we crossed the compound and went through a large, solid gate that opened onto a very large courtyard similar to what I imagined the interior courtyard of Buckingham Palace to be like. People were standing talking or walking round in small groups. There was no greetings, only mild curiosity as we were led up a few steps just inside the gate and into a fair-sized room, our home for the night. To greet us was what I took to be a typical British cavalry officer in casual dress: a fawn camel-hair three-quarter length

101

coat. Equally casually he briefed us on the daily routine.

Except for morning roll-call, life in this camp would be as good or as bad as each individual cared to make it. The address when writing home was POW camp Offlag IVC (4C). Although an officer's prison, there were no special duties for other ranks sent there. At daily roll-call, as there were so few of us, we would assemble just inside the gate while the officers lined up in the courtyard. Each evening, the cavalry officer briefed us on the latest battlefront news.

It was my first real POW camp, and it took me about a week to settle down, find my way around, and take note of the view from each window available to me. It was a very large building, less than half full, perched on the side of a hill with a rock formation that lent itself as a substantial support to its foundation. Its steep face was its primary defence. Rumours that successive POWs had burrowed through its thick walls to gain access to the offices and stores became more fact than fiction as time went by. The question I always asked myself wherever I found myself incarcerated, was which way does one go in the event of a bomb dropping on or near the prison? This place, it was jokingly said, would collapse like a pack of cards because of its walls being hollowed out. Having had some experience during the bombing of London where buildings did collapse to form heaps of rubble, I recalled a remark from a girlfriend who lived there – 'I sleep fully dressed; it's not nice to be found in just a nightie'. It was good advice and had been practised by me ever since my capture.

The room to which many of us were assigned faced south-east, overlooking the town of Colditz with its bridge that straddled the river Mulde or one of its tributaries, and where small-town daily life went on. The virgin snow that covered the November landscape, meaning that all grazing animals had been brought to shelter among the houses, highlighted pockets of activity. One in particular, when a horse was brought out daily to exercise on a lunge rope; any movement on the outside became the subject of discussion for us penned up in the Shloss above. It was these little scenes that gave some meaning to this small market town.

The casual cavalry officer (CCO) also organized lectures, debates and other cultural activities, that appeared on the 'What's On' board, and attracted 50 per cent of the POW population, among whom were many from the UK's upper crust, ably suited to contribute an informed opinion. The debates offered an opportunity for the junior officers to ridicule them, as they were distinctly hostile to the aristocratic layer incarcerated within those walls, and thus added zest.

I recall one debate, 'If Britain became a Communist Country, what would become of the monarchy?' This was held in a spacious room, and every chair was occupied, every window sill squatted on or stood on, and every inch of floor space taken up. This was made all the more poignant as relatives of the monarchy were present!

An example given by a guards officer ('An American correspondent who was said to have asked a guardsman why he put up with his officers, replied, well, they're different to us') brought howls of laughter and ridicule. Side debates continued in which I became involved in officer/NCO relations and asked a similar question. My answer was a simple one. As a technician, rank was not important. I found most regular officers ignorant of the technical advances currently in use. This set off a prolonged discussion about comparative qualifications that went on until dark.

Attending maths, English and language classes occupied a few hours of my day, together with talks on restaurant management and one given by Jack, the Rhodesian sergeant, on life in Bulawayo. One evening a brilliant play called *Utopia* was performed, set in the English countryside, and many Germans attended. But life, no matter where, has its mundane chores essential to the well-being of the world of prisoners as a group, and internal security was one. It didn't take long to realize among the host of activities there must be some that were strictly illicit. An example was the information we received each day from the battle fronts. The German commandant knew a radio existed but didn't know where. His attempts to find out were hampered by a network of POWs

103

posting themselves at strategic places at all hours of the day, using the code-word 'Goons-up' whenever a patrol or humble guard came in sight. The placid calm never failed to impress me as the sound of 'Goons-up' circulated throughout the building; everyone just kept doing whatever they were engaged in as if they hadn't heard.

Although the majority of prisoners were from the UK there was a sprinkling of Australians and New Zealanders, among whom was Captain Upton, VC and bar, which he had been awarded in Egypt's western desert. There was a Canadian, Colonel Merrit, VC awarded for action at the raid on Dieppe. There were three American officers, one Rhodesian sergeant, one British Brigadier General, three sergeants, and a private who were all connected with executive operations. There was Wing Commander Bader, a legless British pilot, and many who were prominent in British society circles. The place was a university of a kind, vibrant with ideas for the future. Everyone was going about the business of living and contributing to make life as normal as possible under the circumstances.

Christmas was approaching and the urge for strong drink became an obsession among many who contributed dried fruit, sugar, and any other ingredients from their Red Cross parcels to ferment to make a concoction aptly named 'Jungle Juice'. When distilled, as some was, it was known as 'Hooch'. There were great expectations as each group vied to make the best, but for this we had to wait and see.

In the meantime I had been landed with the job of collecting and distributing extra potatoes for our group. These items were by courtesy of the camp forage party, believed to be a group of RAF officers skilled in crawling within the crevices of the walls. Among them there existed a locksmith able to open any lock put in front of him.

The potato and coal store opened onto the courtyard and was periodically topped up. To get at them there needed to be another access known only to the forage party. The goods being hauled out were some distance from our quarters and were collected by coal buckets. Oddly enough, the buckets holding around fifty pounds were identical to those used in UK army camps. There was an element of risk when collecting or returning as it took two to carry the stuff past at least one guard. However, if the guard had been stationed at the prison for any length of time little notice was taken of internal trading.

The idea was to take the bucket quarter-full of coal. On arrival we tipped out the contents, filled the bucket with spuds and replaced the coal. There had to be a time lag before returning so as not to arouse suspicion. On one occasion I noticed an officer at an easel and strolled over to the window and looked down on the same scene that had attracted my attention from the window below. The artist was a Captain in the Scots Greys, who had captured the snowy scene with its exercise ring, where the horse, on a lunge rope, had worn a perfect circle in the snow as it walked, trotted or cantered each day. We discussed the scene. The horse was no 'nag', and we concluded it probably belonged to the local commander. (Later, after the war, I saw that painting on display. The artist – the Laird of Elphingstone!)

It was really getting cold now. Each morning the courtyard was covered in frozen snow. Some of us had no overcoats but this was soon remedied. Where they came from, I didn't ask. Some Germans somewhere were wearing the parka's our mission arrived in; this was a fair exchange.

Cold as it was, this did not prevent the majority from walking round the yard for exercise, their threadbare uniforms covered by blankets and wearing an assortment of headgear to prevent losing body heat – a precious commodity when calorie intake is low. They came and went, so too did the cats as they sat in a doorway watching the coming and going of the inmates. One would very gently extend a paw, touch the snow, then scamper off and disappear through another door. They patrolled the labyrinthine corridors controlling the denizens that foraged by night. Whatever kept them alive did them proud, for they looked well.

As each POW was his own practitioner, the daily ration plus the contents of the weekly Red Cross Parcel was for his own survival – cooking stoves were available. There were, at times, coal shortages. Many made their own highly efficient contraptions that gave off intense heat fed by little balls of paper or cardboard at the same time drawing down the smoke to be reburnt. These smokeless cookers were made from empty food tins, a by-product of the Red Cross parcel, and fuelled by remnants of the Red Cross parcel boxes, and they became a boon to creative cooking.

With the approach of Christmas, our CCO informed us on one of his evening visits with news, that the German commandant had been approached and asked if a little extra coal and meat for Christmas Day could be provided. He didn't say yes and he didn't say no, but his staff would do what they could under the circumstances. The circumstances, we all knew, were really rough on Gerry. He was being pressed from all sides, and this Christmas was not going to be, for them or us, one of peace to all mankind.

All the while the Hooch and Jungle Juice hopefully gained strength as the days to Christmas dwindled. There was little to look forward to, though little things became important, equally to those who possessed estates as those who lived in a council house. Prison was a great leveller, whether walking round the courtyard in small groups debating the prospects of ever getting out alive, or standing at a window looking out over an alien world while dreaming of another called home. Life itself, at this moment in time, was very uncertain. It was the American and Russian governments that would call the tune at the end of this shindig. There would be no hostages to exchange.

Christmas Day dawned with a head count in the snow-covered courtyard where we were held for as long as it took the guards to search the rooms. These Germans were not sadists, just people doing a job within the confines of their own limitations. Later that day, privates and generals would share the contents of a large copper, in which a sort of goulash would be boiling. Whatever it turned out to be it was the sharing that really gave the meaning of Christmas. As the cook ladled out the stuff, I stood in the queue next to

106

Princess Elizabeth's cousin. The meat was sparse but not immediately recognizable, as it slopped into my tin bowl and was taken to my room. I noticed a knuckle in my spoon as I ate; though well cooked, the sight of it played on my mind. What was I eating?

During the evening, from several rooms, came individually created culinary masterpieces purporting to represent Christmas cake and other goodies. These were laid out for consumption among bonhomie and laughter, and washed down with Hooch and Jungle Juice that fell short of all expectations. It was all good fun. The party broke into small groups of card players and cliques discussing home interests, but the majority sang popular requests to the accompaniment of a mouth organ until the cold of the night forced each to his bed. By morning roll-call, Christmas for most had been switched off. For myself, the knuckle in my helping of goulash continued to gnaw at my senses. For days I kept a lookout for the prison cats; none appeared. I heard no one remark on their absence. By the seventh day, I knew they had been eaten. I was convinced the knuckle had belonged to one of them; to think the cats had been butchered on Christmas day so that we might live was an odd and disturbing thought.

The approach of New Year heralded nothing as 1944 came to its end.

6

1945: The Last Round-Up

The news from the front lines had all the hallmarks of a gigantic race to the river Elbe and Berlin, between Russian and Allied forces. The Germans faced an overwhelming Russian army from the east, hell-bent on revenge, total surrender and occupation. German army units retreating from the Russian front, despite the difficulties they must have encountered, brought with them prisoners of war, thousands of them. Oflag IV C (in Colditz) during January 1945, received around 1,300 French officers. Later, a group of Polish officers arrived among whom were General Bor Kamarovski, leader of the Warsaw uprising against the German army of occupation.

To accommodate the new arrivals, the theatre, debating hall and several other rooms that had been used for many purposes in this university prison, were converted. The comfortable routine, temporarily disrupted, was not abandoned. The urge to meet, to discuss and pursue individual interests overcame all difficulties. Thankfully the small map room remained as it was, a window of information for all to see. Little pin flags representing the nations taking part were moved each day by someone who certainly had his ear to the ground. Even the prison guards were to be seen studying the map.

During the rearranging, our group of NCOs was billeted high in an attic room with a window facing roughly south-east, commanding a panoramic view of a rolling landscape with Dresden in the distance. In practical terms this new position meant, in the event of a bomb landing on the prison we would have a lot farther to fall.

108

As Allied bombing appeared to have been stepped up, and was certainly nearer, stray bombs landed on the edge of the town below. Screams could be heard from where I stood. The vibrations passed through the prison walls. Nothing crumbled.

Next morning, I visited the map room. The map was being brought up to date. I asked the plotter who got it last night. His reply was casual. Without turning his head he said: 'I'm not sure; either Leipzig or Chemnitz, or both. It's Dresden next'.

Colditz town was situated in a triangle, Dresden to the east, Chemnitz to the south and Leipzig to the north-west. By the end of January, morale among the guards was distinctly sinking, as bombing continued to be concentrated in the area. But somehow, even with the end in sight, the guards continued to perform their duties rather than abandon them. Was it pride that delayed the shame that must follow surrender? I liked to think that they were protecting us from ourselves if the gates were opened.

Early in February at a news briefing it was reported that at the Black Sea port of Yalta the three heads of state (America, Britain and Russia) had met, in the words of the CCO, to 'carve up Germany'. It was believed and feared that the Russians had insisted on the bombing of the three largest cities in eastern Germany to take pressure off their forward troops. The casual words 'It's Dresden next' came true in mid-February. As I have mentioned, I had taken to dressing before turning in for a night's sleep. On this particular clear night the drone of bombers about midnight was particularly prolonged. The first signs that Dresden was going to be hit were bright flares that could be seen descending over the city.

For the next two hours I watched the city burn. A city that had escaped the real war its own government had started. A city in which its inhabitants must have witnessed the passage of Nazi victims during the last five years, without any signs of protest. A few minutes in Dresden's marshalling rail yard gave a clear indication to me that it had been used extensively for the transit of prisoners or victims of the Nazi regime.

What seemed to be marker flares were followed by wave

after wave of bombers unloading their bombs on the burning city. Flames leapt, as I watched, then died to be rekindled by yet another wave. Poor sods; sorrow was all I could muster. I recalled a bombing raid on London in 1941 while passing through; the helplessness of those on the ground as hell rained down, scattering to the underground platforms, to shelters to ride out the raid. Next morning, emerging from a cellar of a large building, a sulphurous cloud hung above the burned and shattered houses. That part of London was empty of people. I skirted a colossal hole in the road as I sped towards Victoria station, hoping the underground network was still intact. My destination was Kings Cross station, where I hoped to catch a train to York and report to my place of work at Northern Command Communication Centre. Nothing was certain, except if you were late for duty, you were sure to get a reprimand. That was a long way back, but unforgettable. It was taken as an inevitable part of the war.

My attention was drawn back to Dresden. In an instant something like the rising sun appeared on the horizon, slowly getting bigger to form a complete semicircle not unlike an early morning summer sun on a clear day. It enveloped what I took to be part of the marshalling yard and west side of the city. As it grew the white brightness at its centre, although 25 to 30 miles away, lit up the room. I called to the others to come and see it, more for a second opinion than anything else. No one stirred. 'We've seen it all before,' was the only response from a person drowsy with sleep. Most in the room had been in the bag (prison) for three or more years. I made no further attempts to arouse interest but stayed at the window trying to figure out what had caused this huge inferno that now appeared to engulf the west side of the city. To the east of the city reddish flames could be seen. I thought it could only be a high octane or rocket fuel dump or large bomb that had exploded.

It must have been 3 a.m. before the flickering, whitish flames died. On the east side, the reddish-coloured flames from the bombing were dying out. I turned in and tried to sleep.

Later reports describe fire-balls created by wind. The rising sun-like ball that I witnessed was not created by wind but by some type of explosion, a fact the Germans have never admitted and the British public never believed. I do not dispute the heat and wind did produce fire-balls but not of the dimension or the colour described.

On my way to morning roll-call, passing a guard, I said, 'Dresden?' Dejected and head bent, he nodded, then said, '*Der krieg ist fertig*' (the war is finished).

As the last clumps of snow lingering in corners of the court yard got smaller more inmates were coming out to exercise. Among our number was a civilian internee who claimed for himself a manhole cover in the courtyard on which to stand during roll-call. He had no wish to be anything other than an internee. He once gave a talk on his work as an international correspondent based in Riga on the Baltic sea. He escaped the Russian advance into the Baltic states, only to be caught up in the German advance into Norway in 1940.

With so many now occupying this country manor house that had acquired the status of a castle, our only civilian started an exchange and mart enterprise. The French and the Poles, believe it or not, did not qualify for food parcels, but their coming provided a fertile field for a fairer distribution of food.

My trousers were threadbare at the knees. Within two days he had procured a pair from a French army officer. The cost: a tin of cheese half for him, and half to the French Captain who I eventually met. He was from Tunis, a schoolmaster that had been a prisoner since 1940. We met in the courtyard to discuss the progress of the war and what arrangements were being made to evacuate the castle. I knew some officers were working on how to contact the Allies, as I had been approached to join a team if it became necessary to make radio contact, but I didn't think any firm measures had been taken.

Lectures and talks continued as did language classes, but the most important to those from the UK was the arrival of a copy of the Beveridge Report on the possibility of a National

111

Health Service. That brought about group discussions and heated debates that took preference over much of the planned talks for March. Copies of the Report could be borrowed. I read it and was very impressed by the far-reaching effect it could have on the people of the UK as a whole.

April brought sunshine and hope. The air-raids on Dresden, Leipzig and Chemnitz together with the relentless steam-roller effect of the advancing Allied armies was crushing all obstacles the German army could put in their path. News bulletins indicated that the American Ninth Army was heading our way. The Russian army group under Marshal Koniev had turned north on the east side of the River Elbe, to reach Berlin from the south. Marshal Zukov approached from the east. By agreement, the Americans stopped on the west side of the River Elbe. Subsequent news readings were precise. Anyone interested enough could forecast the exact day the Americans would arrive in Colditz as part of their mopping-up operations.

I am not sure of the exact date the first Americans were sighted, and can only guess it was 12 April. Most inmates were in the courtyard or at the various windows, hanging out national flags. I don't think they would have done much to prevent the odd shell, as I discovered while searching the very top rooms for a better vantage point. A shell burst on the hill-side some 50 yards from where I stood. It could have been a parting shot, as the German troops in that area were surrendering. There was no way of telling or accounting for human behaviour; your life was in your hands.

I contemplated this in a room where some prisoners had been busy making an aeroplane, something like a Tiger Moth. It was no more than a toy, its skin of blue and white check cloth, similar to tablecloth material used in cafés. They had obviously made it to pass away time.

Looking across the shallow valley, three tanks had emerged from a strip of woodland. Their target, a line of about ten newly built family houses jutting like a spur into a field. I watched the first three being demolished, all three tank guns focused on one at a time. Each house collapsed like a pack of

112

cards. The people of the town had got the message.

Returning to my room to get a better view of the town itself, there was a mortar manned by three Germans trying to mortar bomb the bridge. In response to their efforts, six mortar bombs, from the American side, landed very near them, and some of the lads cheered. The Germans waved as if to say 'goodbye' and beat it, leaving their mortar behind.

Along the east side of the river that ran through the town, American troops were now entering in their jeeps. Reaching the bridge that spanned the Mulde, the occupants rounded up a number of civilians and made them walk across to the other side and back again before they, themselves, attempted to cross. These soldiers came up the hill and threw open the prison gates. The German commandant was giving instructions to his guards in an attempt to make a formal hand-over. An American caught him by the back of his collar saying, 'Hey bud, your days of giving orders are over', and at the same time pushed him towards the group of German guards being penned up.

The Americans were from the 69th New York Division and had set us free. There was no fuss. We were served meals by the Germans. There was no ordering about, just broadcasts. You were on your own to do as you pleased. A day later we were informed transport would assemble in the town the next day and would leave at 10 a.m. Crowds of German civilians were there, and a lady caught my hand, asking me to try and find her husband, Willie Teal. All she knew was that he was in POW camp number 44. I made inquiries, but no one wanted to know.

The Americans took us to a large aerodrome. Once again instructions were given through loudspeakers as to where to collect blankets, when the evening meal would be ready, etc. It was dark, and a light had been suspended from a pole and shone down on a makeshift kitchen consisting of a large copper of boiling water into which cartons of tinned food were tipped. An American soldier, armed with a large ladle, called out, 'Hot-stuff, Hot-stuff'. A few yards away stood another calling, 'Cold-stuff, Cold-stuff'. The tin of 'hot-stuff'

113

was a lucky dip, anything from curry to Irish stew. In each tin of 'cold-stuff' was a pat of butter, cheese, five biscuits, toilet paper, a few boiled sweets and five cigarettes. Hot and cold tins were clearly marked with a disposal instruction to the nearest bin provided. Several thousand were served within an hour. We had a lot to learn from the US army in the handling of large numbers with minimum controllers.

The next morning we boarded a Dakota aircraft to be flown to England. I had no idea where we landed but were shepherded to a decontamination centre, from which I emerged with a new uniform, complete with stripes and badges, having given details of the last unit I had been in before capture, and was allocated accommodation for one night. Our first meal was one to remember; tablecloths, bright clean knives, forks and spoons, everything was done to bring us back to civilization, including a cabaret!

There was a room set apart for soldiers to telephone home, with ample stationary to write as well. I sat down and viewed this hive of happy industry. Only then did I realize I had no one to write to, or home to call my own. My brothers and sisters had long since abandoned the home we had, to escape the drudgery that existed on English farms. There were new horizons on which I had set my sights; I was determined to pursue them.

We were all sent on 28 days leave. I gave my address as the Union Jack Club, Waterloo, London – a sanctuary for homeless soldiers where I had stayed on my return from India in July 1939.

At the end of my leave, I received instructions to report to barracks in Southsea, near Portsmouth. No matter how hard I tried I could not get back into the swing of military life. Sometime in July I saw an advertisement in the *Echo* placed by the university of Southampton offering a course in marine radio. My application was accepted, but my problem was getting permission to attend the course. Trying to find my way through the official channels was taking too much time; too few cared. I took the advice given to me by Captain Suarez of the US army while languishing in a German prison:

'If you want any job, go see the man at the top. He is the only one who can say yes or no'.

That is what I did. I went to the COs office and requested permission to talk to the Colonel in private. The time was opportune – he had nothing to do and was willing to listen. To my surprise, when I had finished he said, 'What will you do if I turn down your request?'

'Well Sir, firstly I would go and see my Member of Parliament. Secondly, if he refuses to intervene I will take my grievance to the *Echo*. In any case I will enrol with the university on the first day of the course.'

'You are very determined, it would be fruitless to try and stop you. You can't stay here. Off-hand, do you know of any convenient signal unit?'

'Yes sir, there is one at Maresfield camp near Uckfield, Sussex.' (This was very near where my father had a farm.)

*

On arrival at the university as part of probably the first intake after the war, the ravages during the last five years were all too evident, but learning had obviously continued on a low budget. Work that had started five years ago, and stopped at the outbreak of war, was now crumbling as were the piles of bricks and other materials that had spent the last five years on the site.

The rooms allotted us were prefabricated. My fellow students were, as expected 16- to 19-year-olds, and demobs 25 to 30 years old. I shared the same lodgings with two from the latter group. You had to pay for the required books yourself. Tuition fees were in the region of £3 10s per week, lodgings 30 shillings per week. The tutor informed me that grants were available but that took time. I finally managed to get funding but not before I had passed my exams and been in work for a year.

My stay at the university depended on my ability to pay my fees and lodgings. With current earnings plus back pay, I had calculated, my cash would run out in nine months. By then, I hoped to be demobilized and earning my living with the piece of paper saying I was qualified to maintain communications on land and at sea. This would have to do for the time being; my aim was to be qualified to work on civil airliners. The Air Ministry hadn't got round to setting any required standard but through the grapevine came noises that they were working on it.

Fortunately, a like-minded student, Toby Goss, in the same lodgings, made a good companion. Together, we studied each evening except Wednesdays, an evening reserved for socializing. For spare cash at weekends I made up Christmas-tree lights and sold them round the town. Just before the Christmas break the army sent me a cheque for eighty three pounds as a gratuity payment for six years war service. It was no big deal but it helped my social life.

As I hadn't called on my new unit, Christmas seemed a good time to do so, and I set off, arriving at the guardroom at Maresfield Camp. The corporal called from the veranda: 'Name sarge?' and that was it. High Hurstwood was about a mile away; I knew several families there from my boyhood days and set off on foot to the place I hadn't seen since 1935. It was a small village, and to my surprise most recognized me, inviting me in to their homes for a chat. In fact, I stayed on until the first week of January 1946.

Returning to Southampton, the third student did not show up. In March Toby and I decided to apply for employment with the Air Ministry, Admiralty, the Post Office and the Ministry of Defence, all potential employers recommended by our tutor. By return of post came application forms which we studied. Toby applied to the Admiralty; I chose the Post Office mainly because it listed girls. I was desperately keen to have a home of my own, something I had never known during my 29 years of living. For qualifications, I wrote down: 'almost certain to obtain my PMG1'. We took our exams in May, and I passed PMG 1st Class.

I received instructions that my demobilization was due and to report at the demob centre, where I happily handed in my uniform and in return got fitted out for a civilian suit, every thing from socks to a hat. The last thing to be given me was a form to claim any medals due to me. After four days I decided to tear it up and make a clean break; I really had enough memories to last me the rest of my life.

I did join the Post Office Wireless Service, met and married the girl who worked with me intercepting diplomatic radio traffic from around the world. It was magic. In the meantime, I studied, sat and passed the Air Ministry exams to serve as aircrew. In 1947 joined British Overseas Airways Corporation (BOAC) as a Flight Radio Officer. Together we bought a home near Reading in Berkshire. The tailor who measured me for my uniform, by then I had earnt three gold stripes, turned out to be an ex-teleprinter operator I had trained in 1939. It was a pleasant half hour talking of things gone by.

My first duty was with BOAC's Four Line, operating flying boats from Southampton's 'Birth 50' to Hong Kong and Shanghai. Reporting for duty at the docks, a voice called. 'Sergeant Robinson'. Turning, I came face to face with a dishevelled, unwashed person whom I recognized as the man who had taken the boots off a dead German officer in the western desert. Now he was down and out. I was deeply affected, I could do no more than give him a half crown to get himself a meal. What had happened to this once smart young man, I'd never know.

Although the war was over, new ideological wars were starting. China had been taken over by Communists, and the national government had fled to Formosa. Hong Kong was spared, and its population doubled overnight. All through Asia, to the eastern edge of Europe, was a cauldron of dissension.

My next assignment was pioneering civil airlines across Africa, where traders from the Middle East were able to reach areas in Africa as never before. Muslims too were able to move across Africa in comfort and reach Mecca in one piece. Nations in west, east and central Africa wanted independence and West African Airways (a subsidiary of BOAC) played its part in speeding up the process. The British authorities in the

Gold Coast town of Accra imprisoned the leader of the People's Party. A year later he was released as Prime Minister and ousted the remnants of the British Raj, during which time the global cold war was getting colder, and I received papers telling me I had been put on the 'Z' reserve in the event of war. My wife and family were in Africa, probably the safest continent on this round mud-ball. The scare passed over but the remnants stayed for many years.

Returning to England in 1952 I found a nation still on wartime rationing with coupons for almost everything. For 11 years I served BOAC through a period of national and global unrest, and witnessed the disintegration of the British Empire. Then I served a further two years as an engineer on Britain's missile project. A relatively futile project, insane in nature, without any sort of job satisfaction; I resigned in 1960.

My wife and I bought a farm to get away from urban strife, to rear our family and become our own masters on our own patch of land in Sussex.